GOLF
CLINIC

GOLF CLINIC

▶ DIAGNOSIS ○
○ TREATMENT ◀
▶ & OUTLOOK ○

For all the common golfing problems

Written by Lewine Mair
Edited by David Davies

PAPERMAC

First published 1989 by
PAPERMAC
a division of Macmillan Publishers Limited
4 Little Essex Street London WC2R 3LF
and Basingstoke

Associated companies in Auckland, Delhi, Dublin, Gabarone, Hamburg, Harare, Hong Kong, Johannesburg, Kuala Lumpur, Lagos, Manzini, Melbourne, Mexico City, Nairobi, New York, Singapore and Tokyo

ISBN 0-333-47439-2

A CIP catalogue record for this book is available from the British Library.

Typeset by Lineage Ltd, Watford, Herts
Originated, printed and bound in Hong Kong by
Regent Publishing Services Ltd

The authors

Lewine Mair was an English junior golf internationalist who, having played her part in defeating France in an unofficial senior international at Royal St George's, was on the verge of full international honours when marriage and the arrival of her first child checked further ambitions.

As a golf writer she worked for many years with Peter Ryde on *The Times*, following both men's and women's events before taking up her present appointment as Women's Golf Correspondent of *The Daily Telegraph*.

Besides a husband who has represented his country at both rugby and cricket, Lewine Mair has two daughters who play tennis at a national level.

David Davies, Golf Correspondent of *The Guardian,* has been writing about the world golfing scene for almost a quarter of a century. In addition to covering all the leading events in both men's and women's golf, and travelling around 100,000 miles a year, he has pursued his hobby, playing golf, in places as far apart as Kathmandu and Death Valley, California.

Using *Golf Clinic*

Like all good ideas, this book is basically simple. Underlying it is our conviction that to be truly useful, a golf instruction manual should not have to be *waded through*. One simply does not retain advice, especially on a physical game such as golf, by having it thrown at one page after page.

By all means browse through the book and see what interests you; but above all, use it to tackle problems and bad habits as they arise.

As you would expect, the book is in sections covering long shots (FROM TEE TO GREEN), short shots (ROUND THE GREEN) and putting. There are also sections on hazards, including weather, mental approach and advanced play. There are back sections on the rules and practice; and a glossary. If in doubt about where in the book to find a problem, first consult the contents list which follows; the index, however, may be just as useful.

One exception to the recommendation to use the book as problems arise is the section on basic techniques. It is short, but essential reading.

Contents

BASIC
TECHNIQUES

Basic techniques

The teaching professional, Ken Adwick, once told of how his elderly father's idea of a good practice was to sit and think. Old Father Adwick was 83 at the time and, in winning his age-group in the 1975 Seniors at Longniddry, contrived a round of 78 over that tricky seaside course.

The lesson here – one of sitting and thinking – is not just for octogenarians but for golfers of every age anxious to get the most out of the game.

Think first. Take time to check that your swing is built on well-laid foundations which, in due course, will allow it to stand up to such things as wind, fatigue and pressure.

Grip

The first point to ponder is the grip. You will probably have chosen from the overlapping grip, known as the Vardon grip; the interlocking grip; or a two-handed hold on the club. The overlapping grip is the most popular. Above all, you should discover the position which allows you to keep a secure hold on the club throughout the swing and to whip the clubhead precisely into the ball. In order to find, or check on, the proper alignment for the left hand – and this will apply to whatever grip you have chosen – set the club up behind the ball, with the face pointing in the direction you want the ball to go.

With the back of the hand facing the target, grip the club as in the illustration, making sure that the sole of the club is still resting, comfortably, on the ground. In looking down, you should see two to three knuckles, while the 'V' formed by thumb and forefinger should be pointing between your chin and right shoulder.

For the sake of those who are still in two minds as to which grip is best, the overlapping grip is arrived at as follows:-

When introducing your right hand, settle it below the left in a manner which, were you to open both hands, would have the palms facing one another. Now slide the right hand up to let the little finger slip over the forefinger of the left hand and lie snugly in the channel between the index and third fingers of your left hand.

In the interlocking grip, the same little finger intertwines with the first finger of the left hand (see illustration). Where the two-handed grip is concerned, make sure that the hands settle closely enough to perform the all-important task of working as one unit.

Familiarize yourself with your grip. This is an area of the game on which Ben Hogan recommended half an hour's practice per day in a golfer's early stages or when a player is returning to the game after a break. It is essential to ensure that the last three fingers of the left hand have a secure hold on the club.

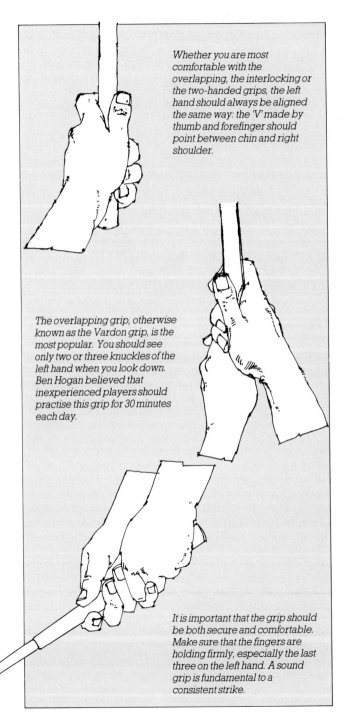

Whether you are most comfortable with the overlapping, the interlocking or the two-handed grips, the left hand should always be aligned the same way: the 'V' made by thumb and forefinger should point between chin and right shoulder.

The overlapping grip, otherwise known as the Vardon grip, is the most popular. You should see only two or three knuckles of the left hand when you look down. Ben Hogan believed that inexperienced players should practise this grip for 30 minutes each day.

It is important that the grip should be both secure and comfortable. Make sure that the fingers are holding firmly, especially the last three on the left hand. A sound grip is fundamental to a consistent strike.

If you play with a good grip, everything else you do right will be rewarded. If your grip is a bad one, you are liable to have to spend the entire swing making compensations.

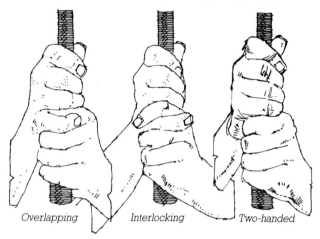

Overlapping   *Interlocking*   *Two-handed*

Stance and set-up

Stance and set-up are no less important than the grip. They are areas in which every golfer, from the humblest amateur to the top professional, can be correct.

To check your address position, stand with your feet together and allow the club to settle on the ground in the position dictated by the sole. Now move the feet apart, but no further apart than shoulder width. In the basic stance, lines drawn across the front of the feet and shoulders should be parallel to that along which the clubface is aiming.

The arms should be hanging down comfortably, while the correct posture can best be achieved by imitating that of a good player (see illustrations). What you must not do, to borrow from the words of Tommy Armour, the famous American teaching professional and winner of the Open Championship in 1931, is stoop, stretch or squat. The left arm and the shaft of the club should be practically in line and you should feel perfectly placed to make a proper body turn.

Greg Norman plays every ball from just inside his left heel, whereas Seve Ballesteros, after hitting anything from a drive to a 4 iron from that position or thereabouts, moves the ball back in his stance. With his short irons, it can even be 5 to 7 inches further back.

If you have reason to suspect that your set-up is badly awry, lie a club across the front of your toes when you are in the address position. From behind, you may well find that your feet were set up to hit very much further off target than

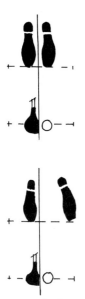

Stance and set-up
*After correct grip, this is the
second essential for a consistent
strike. First, stand feet together,
the club settled behind the ball.
Then move the feet apart, left first
(as above), then right (as
opposite). When driving, aline
the ball with the left heel.*

you would have believed possible.

If someone has pointed out that your stance is flat footed,
it is worth examining what that may be doing to your overall
action. While it is no bad thing to have the left toe turned out
a shade to facilitate the appropriate leg action on the follow-
through, it is not a good idea to have the right toe turned
outward. The correct placement of the right foot – square to
the line of flight – serves to put exactly the right break on
your turn away from the ball on the backswing.

If your right toe is turned out, your hips and shoulders will
swing round to a degree where you will have trouble in
getting back to the ball. Once that happens you can be sure
that much of the power will be dissipated.

Ben Hogan once made the point that, whereas the golfer
who stands flat footed looks from afar as if he could be about
to hit left handed or right handed, the one who has his left
foot turned out looks perfectly placed to pour everything he
has into his shot.

Don't be influenced by those who tell you that you should

stay with your flat-footed stance if that is natural to you. With a little application, your new position will feel as comfortable as the old.

The swing

You should prefer a fuller swing to one which is foreshortened. Most of the top players believe that a fuller swing, provided that it is properly executed, will stand them in good stead for longer.

You will automatically swing far enough, but not too far, if you avoid the following faults:

a collapsing on the backswing
b bending your left arm
c letting go with your hands
d lifting or moving your head

Golfers who feel their swings are getting shorter, particularly as they grow older, should copy the exercise Gene Sarazen recommended for Joyce Wethered when she had stopped playing regularly. Sarazen was one of four men to win all four of golf's major championships; Miss Wethered was probably the best lady player of all time, and the

Keep the swing free, full and yet controlled. The appropriate arc is sometimes compared to that of a cartwheel – it describes a full circle.

Arrows show knee direction resulting from correct weight transfer and ankle movement.

Sarazen exercise which, she said, helped to open out her shoulders at a time when she was apt to get a little stiff, was one of swinging with a specially weighted club every morning.

If you are starting out in golf, you should be aiming to develop both a full swing *and* good control side by side. To help make your action secure, spend time swinging a club to and fro through long grass and hit plenty of practice balls.

To prevent your alignment from getting sloppy, walk up to shots from behind and make a mental note of something – perhaps a tuft of grass – over which your ball must travel.

In settling into your address position, make sure that you are not crouching further and further over the ball. If you do this you will miss out on the necessary extension to the backswing and you will have real difficulty, on the down-swing, in swinging through the ball along the right path.

Stand up to the ball; keep your left arm straight, but not taut; make a full and free turn with the upper body.

Just as a tennis player cannot expect to unleash a hard service if he or she does not make full use of height, so the golfer must make maximum use of physique.

Balance

Sound footwork enables you to stay balanced and to make a full and effective swing. It takes in a correct rolling of the ankles while all the time keeping the knees flexed. On the backswing, the left ankle rolls inwards towards the right foot, with most of the weight transferring to the inside of that right foot.

On the way down, both ankles roll laterally to the left so that the weight gradually moves from the inside of the right foot to the inside of the left. The right heel will lift steadily and naturally on the follow-through. Many golfers do not recognize how important it is that there should be a well-balanced follow-through.

Hector Thomson, the Machrihanish professional who taught former Curtis Cup player, Belle Robertson, used to get the message across to his pupils by saying, "Look good for the camera". A useful image to remember – and one that the successful Mrs Robertson never allowed herself to forget.

Keep the head steady

Moving your head can ruin your swing. It is more important to keep your head steady than any other part of your body, the reason being that a moving head can lead to so much else going wrong. While you might often do better to ignore advice from golfing colleagues, the 'head-up' situation can be spotted even by the most untutored eye.

Jack Nicklaus has said: "I regard keeping the head steady, if not exactly stock still, as the bedrock fundamental of golf". Obviously, it is a matter not just of keeping the head steady but in the right place.

Nicklaus likes to feel that his left cheek is level with the back of the ball. Before he starts his backswing, he moves his chin an inch or so towards the right shoulder.

Since so many golfers appear taken aback when told that they are moving their heads, it is an area which requires frequent checking-up. If you are practising on a sunny day, take the opportunity to position yourself so that the shadow of your head covers a twig or some such object on the ground. On completing the shot, glance back at the shadow to discover if you kept your head still.

These are the fundamentals of the grip, stance, set-up and swing; these, plus staying balanced and keeping your head still, are the basic techniques of golf which you must get right and check at regular intervals. *Golf Clinic's* supremely clear analysis of all the problems which can beset these basics is designed to help you do just that.

Lessons

There has never been a better time to be taking lessons. Most professionals today teach the game in much the same way.

If, for example, you are a junior having lessons from your own club professional and are sent elsewhere through some training scheme, you are unlikely to be upset by the experience. Listen to all professional advice and pick out what works for you.

If you are failing to benefit from lessons, you may not be giving your professional a chance. Are you letting him tell you what is wrong or are you telling him? While you need to explain the area where you are having trouble, leave it to the professional to weigh up your mistakes. If you don't understand what he is saying, ask him to put it another way.

If your professional has not seen you play for a while, you might ask for a playing lesson. That way you can discuss problems as you go round the course. The professional will get a better idea of what you can and cannot do before moving to the practice ground.

Equipment

Try before you buy. You should not contemplate buying new clubs if you cannot try them out. Nowadays there are manufacturers who give professionals trial sets of clubs for prospective purchasers.

You will need to hit shots with each club to see if you and

they are compatible. Never choose a new set on the grounds that you like the feel of a couple of the clubs. Try out each one in turn, checking that feel and lie agree with you. Also, ask your professional to check the swing weights.

Remember, you are spending the money. You should not end up with a set in which, say, the 4 iron feels like a complete stranger among the rest.

Roberto de Vicenzo, the 1967 Open Champion, made the point when he was in Britain for a recent Seniors' event that golfers should look for woods with plain heads. Ones which have some feature picked out he dismisses as fussy and distracting.

Before buying a new club, it is worth looking to see if the face of the club is set square. Many manufacturers aim for a slightly shut face to combat the average golfer's tendency to slice. However, if the effect is overdone, or simply not what you want, ask your professional to make the necessary adjustment. Still worse than buying a club with an in-built draw or hook is to buy one with an in-built slice – but this again can be easily doctored.

If you are buying a new set of clubs, one of the first things you should look for is whether the clubhead sits easily on the ground and whether the clubface is set square. It could be that the driver and the 5 wood lie perfectly while the 3 wood, say, simply does not look right. If you have to adjust your hold on the club in order to have the clubface correctly aligned, that club is not for you. Don't be persuaded otherwise.

You cannot guarantee to set out every time with your swing in proper working order, but you can check that you have the right complement of clubs, together with everything else necessary for a competitive round.

Belle Robertson, who works with the Scottish women's team, recently detailed the list of items she used to carry in her heyday:

Balls; tee-pegs; towel; pencils; markers; rule book; roll of plaster; umbrella; three or four gloves and one all-weather glove stored in a polythene bag; waterproof trousers.

The rule book was one thing she would never be without. "No one," she said, "can hope to stand his or her ground without it – and that applies to everyone, regardless of whether they are playing in a club's third team or a full-scale international."

On really wet days you often find professionals equipping themselves with big polythene rubbish sacks. The idea is to slip them over the top of the bag to stop the rain running down the clubs and on to the grips.

If you are a novice in need of equipment, there is little chance of your finding the right clubs on your own. You need the advice not of a middle-handicap friend, but of a reputable professional.

If you are left handed, don't automatically assume that you will be better off with a left-handed set of clubs. Let your professional watch you swing both right handed and left handed, or even book a lesson in which he or she will have the time to judge more fully on which side your golfing future lies.

This is because it pays in golf to hit against a strong left side. The left-handed golfer playing right handed already has this strong left side and there are many who have deemed this a great advantage.

At the Kristianstad Golf Club in Sweden they automatically ask right handed lady newcomers if they would like to try to play left-handed. The professionals there have come to the conclusion that the average housewife is so weak in her left hand that her right arm is apt to be too dominant when she plays right handed, denying her the chance of hitting through the ball with a straight left arm. This development at Kristianstad is interesting in view of the progress being made by young Swedes.

Having decided between playing right handed and left handed, women golfers should find it relatively easy to select suitable clubs in that there are only a limited number of lines available. Men, on the other hand, will almost always find an enticing and extensive range of clubs. More often than not, they will fall into the trap of picking out a set designed for someone much stronger than themselves.

People are too easily swayed by the name on the head, or by the fact that a certain tournament player was using such and such a set when he won: sound reasons why the restraining influence of an experienced player is all important.

The same obviously applies to youngsters. It is essential that they should not begin with clubs that are too heavy. It is also important that, when he or she begins to play competitively, the clubs are not so poor as to be putting the junior at an obvious disadvantage.

Golf instruction manuals, a positive approach

The golfer who leafs through *Golf Clinic* with the same sense of impending doom as he or she might a medical dictionary is not going to make headway in a game where positive thinking is so essential.

There will be many times when you will need to look no further than this opening section to uncover what is wrong with your game. Grip and set-up are all important: two points always worth checking before starting to look for other answers.

FROM TEE
TO GREEN

Trouble getting set

No questions: Keep your mind clear so that you feel right at the address for a swing which can be repeated automatically.

Diagnosis Your mind is so overtaxed with theories that you have made it impossible, mentally, to achieve an easy, comfortable position at the address.

Treatment It is essential that you have the correct grip, with feet and everything else properly set. However, you must also feel right at the address – and this is something which can be worked on at home as well as on the practice ground. On the tee you don't want to be asking yourself questions about your set-up.

Outlook Watch how top players arrange themselves for a shot. This can be more valuable than observing individual points of technique.

Pro tip What is most impressive about Seve Ballesteros's set-up is his repetitiousness and economy. American writer Ken Bowden says, "I believe that any golfer of reasonable health and strength who could emulate Seve's set-up in all its particulars, then move the club to and fro with, say 75 per cent of his freedom and fluidity, would have one heck of a job averaging much over par".

Skied drives

Above: *teed up too low.*

*Equator of ball level with
top edge of clubface.*

Diagnosis There could be a simple explanation – namely
teeing the ball up too high. If this is so, you will be swinging
under the ball, thereby dispatching it into the clouds instead of down the fairway.

Treatment Understand what teeing up is all about. The
accepted rule is that the ball should be teed up to the point
where its equator is level with the top edge of the clubface.
This encourages making impact with the clubhead slightly
on the upswing.

However, it is not just from teeing the ball up too high that
you get the drive that balloons into the air. The same thing
can happen if you tee it too low, when you are forced into
giving the ball a more descending blow.

Outlook Until you are in a fairly advanced category, get into
the habit of teeing the ball up exactly the same each time to
ensure consistency.

Make sure you have an adequate supply of tees which
feel right for you. You don't want, in mid-round, to have to
borrow a shorter tee when you are used to a long one: it can
undermine confidence. Many professional's shops sell tees
which can only be inserted a certain depth into the ground.
These are worth a try.

Topping

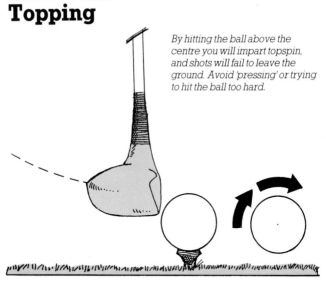

By hitting the ball above the centre you will impart topspin, and shots will fail to leave the ground. Avoid 'pressing' or trying to hit the ball too hard.

Diagnosis The 'top' is caused by the club striking the ball above centre, thereby imparting topspin. Your topped shots will travel in the direction you hit them without leaving the ground.

Treatment Keep your eye on the precise point on the ball you intend to hit and make sure that you keep your head down. One possible cause of your topped shots is that you have developed a sway (see pages 102, 125). Cut down on the movement and, instead of pulling up on the follow-through, make a point of hitting past your chin.

Remember that your hands, at impact, need to be in the same position as they were at the address. Check you are not stooping at the set-up: this posture will encourage extra movement as you seek to 'find' the ball on the downswing.

Outlook You should not have too much trouble in ridding yourself of the occasional 'top'. Remember you are at risk every time you try to hit the ball harder than usual.

Pro tip When most people start golf they despair of getting the ball up into the air. Tony Jacklin, Open Champion in 1969, U.S. Open Champion in 1970, points out that in order to get the ball up, the club has to hit down. "Take something like a 7 iron," he says, "and try to hit a ball into an upturned bucket a few feet in front of you. You'll find it flies over every time."

Slicing

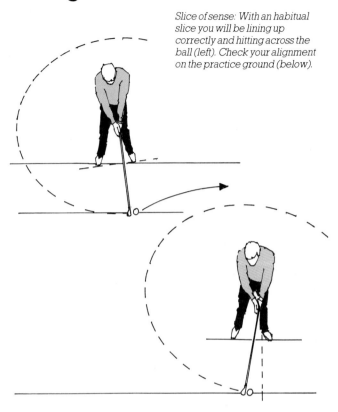

Slice of sense: With an habitual slice you will be lining up correctly and hitting across the ball (left). Check your alignment on the practice ground (below).

Diagnosis You are probably making the common mistake of facing left of the target and coming across the ball – outside to in.

Treatment Prevention is better than cure. Your slice could probably have been avoided had you made regular check-ups on your alignment. Every time you visit the practice ground, make a point of putting a club down across your toes and then standing behind that club to see if you are aiming on target.

If your alignment is in order, it could be that you are throwing your right shoulder at the ball on the downswing.

As Ken Adwick, the teaching professional, suggests, you should feel that your hands are going to brush past your right-hand trouser pocket in the hitting area.

A severe slice may be caused by bad alignment. Take a few days away from competitive play in order to give yourself the chance to get back on comfortable terms with the correct address position.

Smothering the ball

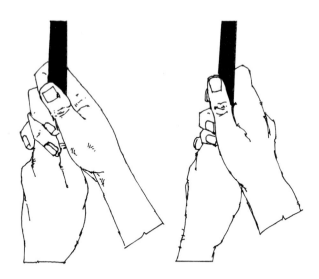

Closed chop: A grip with the right hand under the shaft will make a hook worse.

Get a grip: Check that you are holding the club properly, as above.

Diagnosis This is a close relative of the duck hook, the likelihood being that you are coming into the ball with the face of the driver closed. Both hands could be turned too far over to the right of the shaft.

Treatment Check your grip. See if you need a more open clubface at impact. In setting the hands on the club, ensure that you have no more than three knuckles of your left hand showing at the address.

Check too, that the right hand is not too far under the shaft. If it is, it will be automatically inclined to roll over on to the left on the downswing, thus encouraging a duck hook or, if it is that bit more pronounced, a smother.

Sam Snead, who suffered from a duck hook-cum-smother early on in a career in which he won seven major championships, only got the correct feel in his right hand when he started holding the club "neither in the fingers nor in the palm of the hand but in both. The combination gave me that good feeling of both strength and control".

Outlook Once your grip is sorted out, the clubhead will come into the ball at the correct angle and you will get the necessary elevation.

Hooking

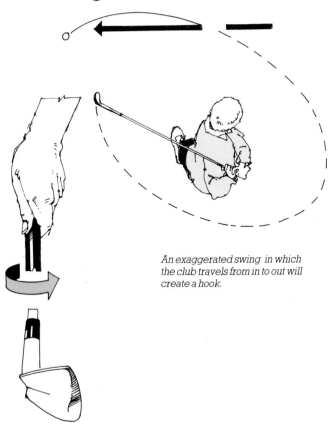

An exaggerated swing in which the club travels from in to out will create a hook.

Diagnosis Hooking is caused by hitting from inside the target line to out, with the clubface turned in. The trouble could be made worse by too strong a grip with your left hand.

Treatment As is always the case when your shots are veering away from the target, you should make a point of checking your alignment. If you find that you are aiming to the right of your intended line, that will have been causing the inside-to-out action through the hitting area.

Where your alignment is not at fault, look down at the grip of your left hand. While you can get away with three knuckles showing at the address, it can be unwise to slip into the habit of showing more.

In making any adjustment to your grip, remember that it is easier to move the hands back to their original position on the club gradually, rather than all at once. You could, in fact, work your way back simply by picking up a club at frequent intervals at home.

Stiff swing

From the hip: A stiff backswing will inhibit your swing, so waggle the club a few times to relax and loosen up.

Diagnosis The unrelaxed or 'wooden' swing is caused by anxiety. Your first move away from the ball has no doubt been very rigid.

Treatment What you need, as Sam Snead, a winner of seven major championships has recommended, is a few waggles of the clubhead to get you loosened up and ready to swing rather than jerk the club away.

Let your hips start the shot, and remember, to borrow from Snead again, "to take things easily and lazily as the golf ball isn't going to run away from you while you are swinging."

Try to reproduce the kind of swing you would make were you aiming to decapitate a daisy or dandelion. In other words, don't get tight simply because you have a golf ball in front of you.

Outlook A few shots on the practice ground can do much to ease the problems of your first tee shot. And the chances are that if you hit a relaxed shot from the first tee, you will feel happier about subsequent drives.

Swinging off balance

Diagnosis It is difficult to overdo the follow-through with your driver because you want your tee shots to be relatively uninhibited. However, an exaggerated follow-through with the shorter irons is unnecessary.

Treatment If you try for a big follow-through with a short club, the chances are that you will automatically set in motion a big backswing. That will cost you something in terms of control.

Remember that the pictures you will have seen of Arnold Palmer at the end of a swing are where he has been using his woods or long irons. His 'all-out' follow-through is not necessarily for you.

Pro tip Jack Nicklaus has advised that the best policy with the shorter irons is to let the club stop at whatever point in the follow-through it "runs out of steam".

Off-balance at the top

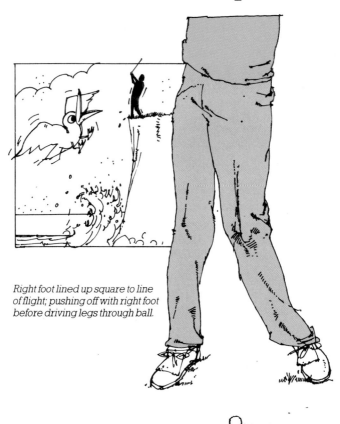

Right foot lined up square to line of flight; pushing off with right foot before driving legs through ball.

Diagnosis Correct weight distribution at the address is no use if you allow all your weight to pour on to the right foot on the backswing. You will have a difficult task in returning the weight to the left foot and in applying the clubhead to the ball.

Treatment One thoroughly effective exercise, devised by American teaching professional Michael Kernick, is to have the impression of playing your shot from a cliff top, with your right foot perilously close to the edge. This should automatically stop you from being too reckless with your weight transfer. (It will help, too, if your right foot is lined up square to the line of flight as opposed to turned out.)

On the downswing, push off with the right foot before driving your legs through the ball. Once you have this feeling and are not merely trying to steady yourself at the top of your swing, your chances of making sound contact will be increased tenfold.

No hit in swing

By the right: Allow the right hand to come into play (right); and make sure that you right shoulder is playing its part, with the right hand and arm acting as guide. Remember to grip firmly with the last three fingers of the left hand.

Diagnosis In adhering to that age-old warning about not letting your right shoulder come into the shot, you may be forgetting about the part your right hand should play.

Treatment Hold the club firmly with the last three fingers of the left hand. Then, letting the left arm and hand act as guide, knock hell out of the ball with the right hand.

Such was the advice Tommy Armour, 1931 Open Champion, once gave to a powerful American footballer who was distressed at being outhit by a slip of a girl. Where the girl in question was using her hands to the full, the footballer was doing nothing to generate speed through the ball.

To make the most of your hands you must give them room to operate and not ruin the effect by moving your body at the same time.

Outlook Many golfers looking for improved action have followed Sir Henry Cotton's tyre bashing routine. Cotton, three times Open Champion, advocated hitting against a tyre with an old club; then turning the club upside down and swishing it to and fro across the inside of the tyre.

Swinging too quickly

Feet together: In practice sessions hit a group of balls with the feet together (left).

Keep it smooth: By concentrating on making a rhythmic takeaway, you will maintain the right tempo (above).

Diagnosis While some people will always swing more quickly than others, you have to remember that too fast a swing puts timing and tempo at risk. For example, Julius Boros, the oldest winner of the U.S. Open Championship, had a rhythm once likened to that of "a lazy man rolling over in bed".

Treatment Take it easy, concentrating, above all, on a slow, smooth movement away from the ball. One well-tried exercise for slowing down is to hit a cluster of balls with the feet close together. This placement of the feet will make a quick swing out of the question if you are to stay balanced.

Start off by swinging the club gently to and fro before graduating to knocking away 30 or so balls with the same easy action.

Outlook In watching the professionals, you will soon see that timing is more important than sheer speed. The average male golfer often finds he can learn more from watching top women than men because so much of their length can be attributed to rhythm.

Slack irons

Count the yards: If you are reasonably sure what distance is left for a shot, you will not have to hold back.

Open, not shut: By keeping your stance open (left), you can keep your hip turn within bounds without reducing your swing.

Contact: Hit cleanly without too much grass between clubface and ball; and strike downwards.

Diagnosis Your grip could be too loose. You may get away with a looser grip off the tee, but the act of hitting the ground makes the shock greater in dispatching an iron. Anything other than a firm hold on the club can result in a twisting of the hands.

Treatment By adopting a slightly firmer grip you will achieve a more solid strike and will encourage the more compact swing required for precision iron play. To this end, you could also stand a shade open at the address, thereby restricting the turn of the hips without consciously cutting down on your action.

Don't go overboard when selecting a club to clear, say, a pond guarding the green at a short hole. Work out the yardage you need to make the distance and opt for the iron you would hit under normal circumstances. That way you will not be tempted to hold back on the shot – which can have dire repercussions.

Outlook You will need to spend plenty of time practising your middle irons. It is only once you are hitting them crisply that you will have any chance of becoming a solid striker with the longer irons.

Long iron trouble

5 wood

Diagnosis The long irons, the numbers 1, 2 and 3, are notoriously difficult clubs to play. Unless you are going to play and practise enough to develop that combination of strength and control demanded by the longer irons, you would probably do better to forget them.

Treatment Experiment with a 5 or even a 6 wood. They are great additions to the armoury of those who find it easier to sweep the ball away.

Outlook The more ambitious will derive much satisfaction from learning to use the longer irons, not least because they can be played to such telling effect in wind. However, there is no great virtue in persisting with these clubs for the sake of it.

Pro tip Sandy Lyle will tell you that these are the most difficult clubs in the bag, even for the professionals. On the subject of the 1 iron, a club which no one hits better than he does, Lyle suggests that fear, more than anything else, leads to mishits. "It's only another golf club," he says, "play it like a driver, with the ball forward to about the left heel. That will get if off the ground automatically and there's no need to thrash it, like so many people think they must."

Scooping the ball

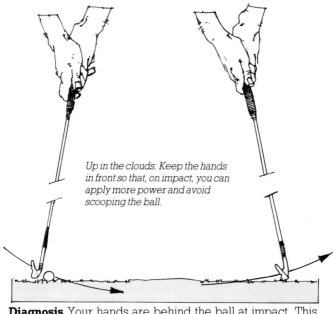

Up in the clouds: Keep the hands in front so that, on impact, you can apply more power and avoid scooping the ball.

Diagnosis Your hands are behind the ball at impact. This could be caused by feeling that you have to lift the ball into the air.

Treatment Convince yourself that the club will do the work of getting the ball airborne.

Similarly, you need to appreciate that, within reason, the more you can get your hands ahead of the clubface on the downswing, the more power you can apply. Closer to the green, the tendency to scoop the ball is still stronger, with the golfer feeling that he must help the ball over a green-side hazard.

Outlook Develop confidence in your clubs and in your ability to hit firmly through the shot.

Pro tip One of the commonest faults of the long handicapper is believing that to get the ball in the air, it has to be scooped. As Sandy Lyle, one of the greatest golfers ever to come out of Europe, says: "You must hit down at the back and the bottom of the ball. The loft of the club will do your work for you. If you need a little extra height with one of the straighter-faced irons, move the ball forward in your stance and play it off the left heel."

Sloping lies

Allow for shots played below the feet to head to the right; those above the feet should go left. Stay cool.

Diagnosis You are failing to make a cool assessment of how the ball reacts on different slopes.

Treatment Whenever you have a shot to play from a sloping lie, with the ball either below or above your feet, you can expect it to fly away from the slope. In other words, the shot with the ball above your feet will tend to fly to the left of target, while the shot with the ball below your feet may veer to the right of where you are aiming.

Balance is essential when you are endeavouring to play off a sidehill lie. When the ball is above you, push your weight on to your toes to stop yourself from falling away from the ball. When the ball is below you, settle your weight on your heels. Your main thought, as you tackle the shot, should be one of maintaining your rhythm.

Outlook If you face a game on a notoriously hilly course you would do well to experiment in practice from sidehill, uphill and downhill lies. This enables you to brush up on how the ball will respond.

Pro tip No fairway is entirely flat and sidehill lies cause confusion for most players. The late Sir Henry Cotton was one of the great shot makers and three times Open Champion. Shortly before his recent death he said: "The important thing when the ball is above you is to keep the weight on to the front of your feet. Leaning forward enables you to keep the arms away from the body and to make a full, free swing. On severe slopes you may have to go down the grip, almost to the metal".

Woods better than irons

Wood

Woods and irons require the same approach and swing. But the longer shaft of a wood will

afford a wider arc than you will get with an iron.

Iron

Diagnosis You are seeing woods and irons as two entirely different shots.

Treatment As Jack Nicklaus has constantly reiterated, the golfer must get it out of his head that he has to make a different swing with the different clubs. The same basic swing always applies. With a wood, you are hitting the ball slightly on the upswing; with an iron rather more on the way down, with the golfer feeling the shot more in terms of a punch.

Clubheads apart, what distinguishes woods from irons is the length of the shaft. The driver will afford a big, wide arc to the swing which will decrease as the golfer closes in on the shorter-shafted, higher irons.

Outlook Even if you do seem to be having more trouble with woods than irons, never devote a practice session entirely to, say, the driver and 3 wood. It is with the shorter irons that you will discover the rhythm you need for successful wood play.

Flying too far

Few club golfers learn to 'read'
the rough. You may get a flier;
your clubhead may be deflected.

Diagnosis Fliers are always likely to occur from rough, but few high-handicap golfers recognize the danger signals. Look out for grass which will come between clubface and ball. This has the effect of cutting down on backspin and making distance and direction unpredictable. The flier, as its name implies, will go further than a shot from a good lie.

Treatment Take one club less than normal. This allows for the flier and is in any case the more inviting tool when you are having to escape from rough. To minimize the amount of grass interfering with the contact, set up slightly open with a view to making a more descending blow on the ball.

Thick grass can deflect your clubhead, so take a firm grip on the club and make a spirited attack on the ball. Letting the clubhead die in the grass is ruinous.

Outlook Learn to recognize how the ball reacts from different lies and in different conditions. All too many golfers play the game without taking account of such things.

Pro tip Jerry Pate won the 1976 U.S. Open at Atlanta Athletic Club with a 5 iron from a typical flier lie. The shot was one of 196 yards and, though everyone felt he did not have enough club, the ball came out like a rocket and stopped 2 feet from the hole.

Wild inconsistency

While you must allow your right side/hand to play a part for length, it is a common fault to have the right shoulder too high. Hold your left side up.

Diagnosis If you are troubled by low, smothered hooks one minute and high shots which land short and right of target the next, you may be using too much right hand in your shots. Most right-handed golfers (who are themselves right handed) have a tendency to use the stronger hand over-much. In Sweden they are suggesting to right-handed women that they should consider starting out in golf as left-handers, but this is probably too drastic an action.

Treatment Check your set-up to see if you are making that mistake – common to so many handicap golfers – of having the right arm too rigid and the shoulder riding high at the address. From that position you are likely to pick the club up too steeply on the backswing before hitting the ball with a sharply descending blow. To come in at such an angle will cause a vicious hook where the clubface is closed, or a high block where the face is open.

Outlook When setting up, raise your left shoulder and check that the left arm is in a line with the shaft of the club. In other words, put the entire left side into a more dominant position and have the right arm relaxed at the address.

Finally, guard against transferring too much weight on to the right foot as you make your backswing.

Incorrect clubbing

Diagnosis You could be among the new breed of golfers who are relying too heavily on yardages.

Treatment Everyone has followed the Americans in terms of setting store by yardages. On U.S. courses you tend to get a uniform bounce of the ball and wind is not an everyday factor; but conditions can be different in other countries.

On British links, for example, there can be too many variables for yardages to be of much use – as many a visiting American has found to his or her cost.

Most professionals would agree that, on such courses, a good caddie can be of more use than a yardage chart; he will know the lie of the land – which of the fairways are relatively soft, or an apron round the green which will be faster than the rest.

Not everyone can afford to have someone shouldering their clubs, but one round with a local caddie can give you a useful idea of what features you can use to your advantage.

Outlook Continue taking yardages, but always remember to look beyond your notes.

Pressing

Leg action: Keep feet and legs working throughout the swing.

Diagnosis You have been getting caught up in too many clubhouse conversations concerning which clubs you are taking where. Once this happens, and you start trying to compete over clubbing, you will find it difficult to hang on to your rhythm and you will lose length.

Treatment Pick out a 7 or 8 iron and head for the practice ground in search of rhythm. But don't set out with the intention of going back to the clubhouse with the news that you were knocking the ball 160 yards or so.

Outlook It will be worth checking whether, in your bid to hit the ball harder, you have not fallen into the trap of bringing too much right hand into the shot.

Note for seniors You are more likely to rediscover lost yards through improved footwork. When you feel your legs getting lazy – and this can happen mid-way through a round – make a deliberate effort to 'think' leg action.

Pro tip Losing length as you get older is, of course, inevitable. But Gary Player believes that you can delay the onset by staying fit, or at least golfing fit. "You must keep flexible," he says. "It only takes a few stretching exercises and you'll be able to keep the swing as long as it was when you were younger. And regular walks help keep off that fat which will also restrict your swing."

Shanking

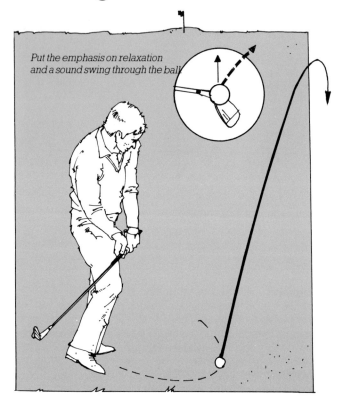

Put the emphasis on relaxation and a sound swing through the ball

Diagnosis There are many possible causes of shanking, some of them almost contradictory. For example, hitting the ball off the socket (the corner where blade joins shaft) can happen to those who stand too far from the ball, and to those who stand too near. The common factor is tension.

Treatment A single shank will be enough to have you worrying so much about trying to hit from the middle of the club that you will find yourself stopping at the ball instead of hitting smoothly through it. By doing this, the problem automatically becomes more pronounced.

Keep hands and arms relaxed and concentrate, above all, on the easy, uninhibited follow-through.

Bobby Jones never hit a shank in his life. But he reckoned that the players most likely to hit such shots were those who employed short backswings with a minimum of hand and wrist movement.

Outlook The cure will be that much faster if you don't make an issue of your shank.

Blind shots

Anxiety to see where blind shots have gone prevents you from keeping your head down. Do your homework or picture a landmark en route.

Diagnosis The usual problem with blind shots is anxiety. Instead of staying down on the shot, the tendency is to pull up too quickly. In junior championships, you will often see youngsters almost running after the ball to see if they have got the direction right.

Treatment The secret with blind shots is to do your homework. If you have a practice round before playing the course for real, stand at a point where you can see both the area where you are likely to be hitting from and the green. If there are no tall trees behind the green on which you can take aim, look instead for an irregularity in the ground a few yards ahead of the ball and line yourself up accordingly. *Don't* follow the example of that Scottish woman internationalist who, faced with a blind second in a recent Spanish championship, walked forwards and decided on a crane operating behind the green for her line. The crane moved while she was walking back to her ball; she missed the green by a long way.

Even if you don't normally rely heavily on yardages, you will need to take them in this instance so that you can have a firm idea in the back of your mind of the distance required.

When it comes to the shot, picture the part of the green you are aiming for and picture, too, a smooth swing.

Outlook Modern course designers rarely include blind shots on their courses, so the problem is diminishing. It should only be a problem, in any case, on the first occasion you play the course, providing the right notes are taken.

Can't achieve extra backspin

What you are looking for is a steeper angle of attack. Swing a little more upright and don't be stiff wristed.

Diagnosis There is no point in striving for more backspin until your basic swing is thoroughly well-grooved. If your swing is not secure, any prolonged attempt to impart extra backspin or, in fact, to play any specialist shot, will upset your game.

Treatment There are plenty of times when a shot with extra bite or backspin can be useful – such, for example, as when you have to clear a large water hazard and hold a green directly to its rear.

To get this backspin, the ball must be hit cleanly, with no grass between blade and ball. The easiest way to achieve this is to have a steeper angle of attack on the ball – something which can be achieved by swinging a little more upright.

In practising the shot, don't be too stiff-wristed. Again, having hit a cluster of balls with backspin, always return to hitting enough regular shots to get back into your habitual groove.

Outlook One reliable way to get the feel of backspin is to watch the professionals in action. Imitation and a real understanding of what you are trying to achieve should combine to help you to learn quickly.

ROUND
THE GREEN

Chipping short

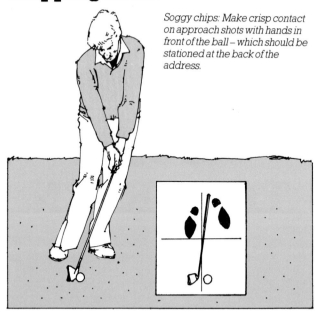

Soggy chips: Make crisp contact on approach shots with hands in front of the ball – which should be stationed at the back of the address.

Diagnosis You are cutting across your approach shots to the green.

Treatment While it is right to have an open stance at the address for the shorter shots, you must guard against having your shoulders pointing too far left of target. If they are, you will inevitably find yourself cutting across the ball to an extent where it will pull up well short of target.

Outlook In altering stance or swing to play a shot that asks for something a little different, remember not to exaggerate. For instance, you don't need to send your pitch shots soaring spectacularly into the air when you have nothing to go over, nor do you need to impart a vast amount of spin when you are playing to a well-watered green.

Pro tip Of all the world's great short-game experts, Lee Trevino is as good as any. From poor lies, he likes to play his little chips with his knees: "Don't just think about your arms and the clubhead. It's more hands, knees and boomps-a-daisy. Slide the knees through the shot, turning them away from the ball as you go through."

No versatility

Learn the running chip by striking it like a long putt, with the weight on the left foot.

Diagnosis This defect in your short game has no doubt become apparent since you started playing on different courses. It will have shown up most where you have switched from an inland course to a seaside links.

Treatment For seaside courses, arm yourself with a running chip. Try using a 5 or 6 iron and, with the feeling of having your weight on the left hip, hit the ball as you would a long putt. Your hands should be ahead of the ball and the ball should be nearer your right foot.

The swing should be one of taking the club straight back and straight through, with the wrists firm to guard against scooping the ball.

Outlook Golfers get by perfectly well using a wedge for all their little shots around the green, especially since modern watering systems have made putting surfaces more uniform than in the past. However, when you do have time to add the running chip to your repertoire, it will pay dividends, not least in windy conditions.

Hopelessly inaccurate

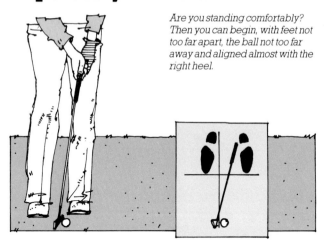

Are you standing comfortably? Then you can begin, with feet not too far apart, the ball not too far away and aligned almost with the right heel.

Diagnosis This is often the complaint of those who fail to settle comfortably over the ball. Many golfers lose control over direction and distance on their short approaches by holding the club too high up the grip, and by standing too far from the ball and/or with their feet too far apart.

Treatment For the little chips, make sure that you have no more than a couple of inches of the club's grip showing below your bottom hand.

If you have been standing too far away from the ball, edge closer. Ideally, you should be not much more than a foot away, while your heels, for shots from just off the apron, should be no more than 8 inches apart.

Outlook You may feel oddly cramped as you adopt your new stance. Unless you have plenty of hours in which to get accustomed to it on the practice ground, you would do better to make this alteration gradually.

Pro tip Gary Player acknowledges how delicate a shot is the chip. He counters his tendency to be anxious, moving his head too soon, by setting out to keep his head still longer than he would for a full shot. Only when the ball is well on its way does he turn to watch the result.

Tufted rough

Grass with care: If you are duffing shots from grass round the green, play them as if from a bunker and open the clubface. Hit through grass and ball.

Diagnosis The rough is hard up against the ball, maybe coming between ball and clubface. This need not be too difficult a prospect if you want to hit a full shot. When you are within 30 or so yards of the green, it is all too easy to get caught between trying to hit the ball cleanly and with the appropriate sensitivity.

Treatment Instead of hitting down on the ball, play the stroke more as a bunker shot; open the clubface a little and hit right through grass and ball. Like bunker shots, these require plenty of practice, for you will want the ball to land softly and accurately.

Outlook You can expect to find more of this kind of rough on seaside courses.

Pro tip Tommy Armour, 1931 U.S. Open Champion, reckoned players can greatly improve their performance out of rough by holding the club with the normal secure grip, *but only that,* and being calmly set on preventing any possibility of twisting.

Putt or chip?

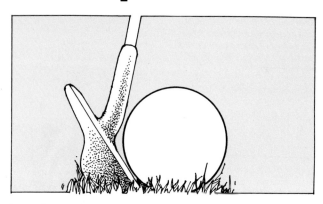

Remember, a poor putt can be less damaging than a poor chip.

Diagnosis This does not have to be a difficult decision. If the grass around the green is short and smooth, you should have no hesitation in employing your putter, or the so-called 'Texas Wedge'. If you are having a bad day with your chipping, bear in mind that a poor putt could be infinitely less damaging than a poor chip.

Treatment You should be able to tell at a glance if the fairway and the green's apron are just too long and/or undulating for a putt to be effective. The combination of the longer grass and your putter having no loft could spell trouble in judging the pace. If this is the case, select a 7 or 8 iron so that you can pitch the ball where you want and be in greater control of its destiny.

You will have seen people putting out of greenside bunkers. This is a useful ploy if there is no lip to the trap. But the good bunker player should always ask himself if he would not do better to play the shot conventionally. Don't be tempted to putt the ball just for effect.

Pro tip Jack Nicklaus finds that the choice usually comes down to common sense. He generally plays the stroke he believes he can do best — in his case the putt — simply because he putts so much more than he chips.

No finger feel

Diagnosis If this is a permanent state of affairs, it could have something to do with your job. People engaged in heavy manual labour, for example, find it difficult to apply touch to the little shots on and around the green. Furthermore, it is notoriously hard to teach people to overcome the fault.

Treatment If you have the choice, don't ask anything too taxing of your hands and arms in the hours leading up to an important match. For example, Bobby Locke, four times Open Champion and a great exponent of the short game, would refuse to carry so much as a hold-all or even lift his clubs from his car. Not because he was worried about injuring his back but simply because he did not want to lift anything heavy prior to handling such delicate things as putts.

Scotland's Belle Robertson would never work in the garden without wearing gloves.

Even driving the car too quickly and with too much tension can wreak havoc with the wrists.

Outlook Remember that what you do in the hours before a game of golf can have no small bearing on what you do on the course. Apart from avoiding physical exertion, you should steer clear of the kind of mental strain you will get from a last-minute rush to make your tee-off time.

Chips not stopping

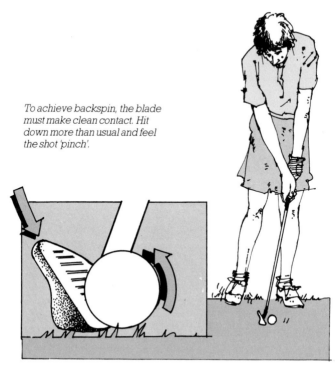

To achieve backspin, the blade must make clean contact. Hit down more than usual and feel the shot 'pinch'.

Diagnosis You are not imparting the necessary backspin. Bear in mind that you don't need to hit checking chips all the time; that a chip-and-run will serve you well enough on most occasions. Where you do need your chips to stop is when you want to land the ball on the green but have only a little green with which to work.

Treatment Before hitting the shot you will need to make sure that the ball is sitting up cleanly so that there is no grass to be caught between blade and ball. Again, look to the landing area. If the green is sloping downhill, no amount of backspin will make your ball pull up by the hole.

If, having taken such things into account, the shot is still 'on', take out your wedge and address the ball slightly back in your stance with the hands just ahead of the ball. Hit down on the ball more than you would in normal circumstances and try to feel that you are pinching it neatly. Remember, the more you hit down on the ball, the more spin you will get.

Outlook It is only by practising over a long period that you can hope to get to grips with this specialized but eminently useful little shot.

PUTTING

Bad streaks

Distracting yourself from the mental rut that causes a bad streak can be as simple as changing your grip – as here, with the left hand at the bottom rather than right.

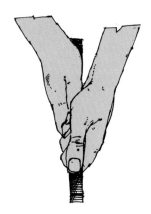

Diagnosis You have got into a rut in which you see yourself missing putts rather than holing them.

Treatment You need something to jolt yourself out of this bad patch. If you have established that there is nothing wrong with your technique, you could try changing the feel of your putter by asking your professional to add a touch of lead tape to the blade. Alternatively, you could alter the feel of the grip, making it a little thicker or thinner. In other words, try anything that will give you the feeling of getting off to a fresh start.

It could be that the putter you are using and the greens you are playing are ill-matched. For instance, you should not use too light or straight-faced an implement on heavy greens. That type of putter is essentially for slick, championship surfaces.

If you do experiment with a second putter, never carry two in your bag at once. This will make you still more unsure of yourself.

Pro tip If, after a couple of weeks, you have still not struck form, it is maybe worth trying a new style, such as putting with your left hand below the right, or changing your putter. Jackie Burke, the former U.S. Ryder Cup captain, never hesitated to change, saying that something different to look at behind the ball made him concentrate harder.

Leaving it short

Swing smoothly: On the follow-through, think only of the face of the putter heading firmly and squarely at the hole.

Diagnosis You probably lack a set stroke and/or a set routine.

Treatment Think in terms of maintaining a firm but equal pressure in the hands. If you grip more tightly with one hand than the other, that can precipitate unnecessary wrist action which could alter the angle of your putter blade.

Let the forearms do the work of taking the club away. Then, as you swing through, think only of the blade heading firmly and squarely at the hole. The essential acceleration through the ball is the result of swinging the putter.

In working on your putting, remember to examine where you are weak. If, for example, you are consistently missing 6-footers, perhaps the solution is to sharpen up your longer putts so that the 6-footers become 3-footers.

Outlook If the practice putting green at your club is poor, you would do better to work on the little putts at home on the carpet. When Michael Bonallack, secretary of the Royal and Ancient, was at the height of his amateur career, he used to buy the family carpets with this in mind.

Pro tip Work out a regular routine that works for you, and stick to it. Seve Ballesteros won the Open at Lytham in 1988 because his brother Vicente reminded him that he had always had his hands very close together, working as a single unit. Over the years they had become loose, drifting apart.

Can't read short putts

*On 3-footers, don't overdo the
business of studying the line.*

Diagnosis You may be making a mistake in trying to read the little ones – that is, those of 3 feet and less.

Outlook Follow the advice of Tommy Armour, the famous American teaching professional and winner of the Open Championship in 1931, and "Forget the dainty business". Instead of trying "to nurse the putt along a curved line, aim firmly at the hole".

Armour used to pick out American teaching professional Johnny Revolta as the master of the short putt. He would walk up to his 2- and 3-footers as if he were saying to himself 'To hell with the line'. If you adopt this attitude you will soon come to see that you have been fussing too much, making the game unnecessarily difficult for yourself.

Pro tip Gary Player, with Nicklaus, Sarazen and Ben Hogan, a winner of the Grand Slam, was notably the best putter of that illustrious quartet. He would hit even the downhill 4-footers hard at the hole, giving them a sharp rap and no follow-through. He was confident they would go in, while if they missed, he never doubted he would hole the one back.

Body movement

Avoid unnecessary movement of the body by locking your left knee inwards in a set position.

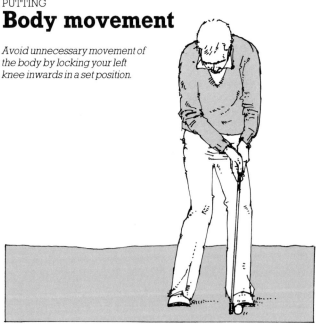

Diagnosis Too much body movement will cost you accuracy. Think of putting as something like threading a needle: you want to keep as still as possible.

Treatment After setting yourself up as you would normally, try turning your left knee in towards the right. The idea is that this deliberate movement will lock you into a set position. Also, to ensure that your arms are not moving unnecessarily, tuck your elbows in at the address.

A little more freedom is acceptable over the long putts, but you should aim to keep the shorter ones as concise as possible. In other words, the stroke itself should be simple, with the golfer cutting out all extraneous movement.

Outlook Luck will always play its part on the green but, as a general rule, you should remember that you will only putt as well as you deserve.

Pro tip Arnold Palmer is one of several virtuoso putters who advocate a knock-kneed stance. He says it firmly anchors the body over the ball and minimizes movement during the stroke.

Off-target from a distance

*Green slopes from
right to left*

Diagnosis You are probably not a hundred per cent sure
whether, in your pre-putt routine, you should be looking up
and down at the hole or at a point to the side of the hole
where you believe you have to aim.

Treatment If your putt is a straight one, you need never be
in two minds as to where you must look. If, on the other hand,
it has a curl on it, don't opt for a target to the side of the hole,
but instead choose a spot on the line about midway between ball and cup.

Having weighed up just how much strength you will need
to apply, let all the rest of your preparations be geared to
putting the ball over the chosen spot.

Outlook The above ploy should be applied to any putt of 10
feet and more. It could make for a more positive approach
in an area where you have previously felt nothing but un-
certainty.

Pro tip As Lee Trevino has said, a
half-way mark will give you
confidence: it is, after all, easier
to hit.

Blown off balance

Diagnosis You are, no doubt, trying to stand up to the wind by widening your stance, hunching yourself over the ball and holding the club rather more tightly than usual.

Treatment A double dose of concentration is needed in windy conditions. You have to learn to forget about the flapping of your trousers and the wind whistling in your ears and think only of getting the ball into the hole.

Outlook Take advantage of windy days to practise the drill suggested below. Not only will it help you to regain and maintain your rhythm, but it will give you the edge in confidence in windy conditions.

Pro tip Davis Love Jnr, who finished joint sixth with Jack Nicklaus in the British Open at Lytham in 1969, has a drill he recommends for putting in wind. Take the putter back the right distance for the length of putt in hand and hold it in that position for ten seconds before swinging through.

Focus all the time on the spot on the ball where you want the putter to make contact; gradually reduce that pause at the back until you are left with your normal stroke.

Wayward from far away

Don't treat long and short putts
the same. See the longer putts as
a miniature version of your
normal swing, with a slight break
in the wrists and the head still.

Diagnosis You may be treating long putts as short ones –
keeping the putter blade square throughout the stroke.
When you are dealing with a long putt, say a 20- to 30-footer,
such a stroke will be too forced and unnatural to incorporate
feel.

Treatment Try to see the swing for a longer putt as a
miniature version of your ordinary swing. Again, don't grip
the club too tightly, for it is essential that your fingers have
the chance to feel sensitive.

There are golfers who try to achieve a total elimination of
hand action from the putting stroke, but the longer putts
should incorporate a slight break of the wrists.

Outlook As in every other stroke, it is crucial with the
longer putts to keep body and head still. Keep your eye on
that part of the ball you wish the putter head to strike.

Negative approach

Think positively: If you are given a putt by an opponent, and are still looking for a practice putt, take it from a different spot.

Diagnosis You are leaving too much to chance. Most people's attitude, when they go out to play, is 'I hope I putt well today'. They have failed to put in the regular practice stint which helps positive thought. You need to be thinking 'Thank heavens, my putting is in sound shape'.

Treatment Don't do anything, in the course of a match, which might detract from your confidence. For instance, if someone gives you a putt, don't attempt to knock it in after the gesture has been made. Instead, move the ball away from that particular spot and take your practice putt from somewhere else.

Outlook When you miss a short putt, don't give away the fact that you are angry with yourself. This will merely serve to convince your opponent that this is an area where he has the edge.

Pro tip Seve Ballesteros, the 1988 Open Champion, has always been the most positive of putters. But for four years, between 1984 and 1988, he forgot the aggression he had when he first came on to the scene, and as a result suffered a majors drought. "At the start of '88," he said recently, "I decided that after I had got the line right, I would go to my ball and hit it very quickly, giving all my attention to making a good contact." It worked.

Too many putts

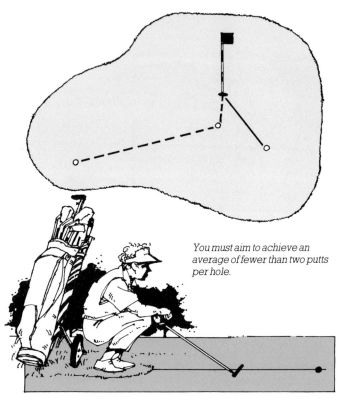

You must aim to achieve an average of fewer than two putts per hole.

Diagnosis You need to regard putting as a certain way to bring your scores down.

Treatment Too many golfers have got it into their heads that if they manage two putts per green they are doing rather well. The fact is that 36 putts per round is a poor tally. In the States, the outstanding putters among the professionals average 24 or 25 putts per round, while Joan Joyce, a former softball player, once had as few as 17 putts in a round of 67.

Bunty Smith, the former British Women's Champion and Curtis Cup golfer, used to maintain that a top-class amateur should be taking no more than 31 or 32 putts on a bad day and that he or she should be aiming at an average of 28 or 29 putts.

Outlook You can afford to set your sights much higher on the greens. Where juniors are concerned, parents should never instil the idea that 36 putts are an acceptable quota.

Start seeing your putter as the most important weapon in your bag. Over a round, you will hit more shots with it than any other club.

Putts seem harder than opponent's

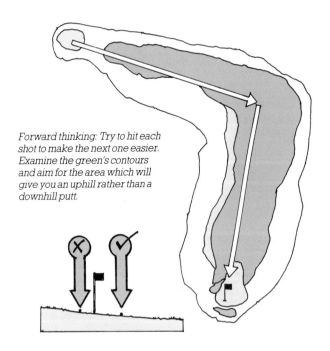

Forward thinking: Try to hit each shot to make the next one easier. Examine the green's contours and aim for the area which will give you an uphill rather than a downhill putt.

Diagnosis If you feel you are getting harder putts than the next person, you are probably failing to think ahead. Every shot you hit should be played with a view to making the next one as easy as possible. To aim blindly for the hole is not enough.

Treatment When playing to a green, you should study the contours and decide which part of the putting surface would make for the easiest putt. If, for instance, the green is sloping from back to front, you would do better to aim for the front of the green with a view to getting an uphill rather than a downhill putt. Obviously, this is especially true where you have a two-tier green with the pin on the lower tier.

When chipping, always think in terms of leaving yourself putts that are straight and, if not flat, slightly uphill.

Outlook The professionals call this course management. Knowing which half or even quarter of a green to aim for, regardless of where the pin is situated, ranks highly among them as a way of getting safely round a golf course.

Lines conflicting

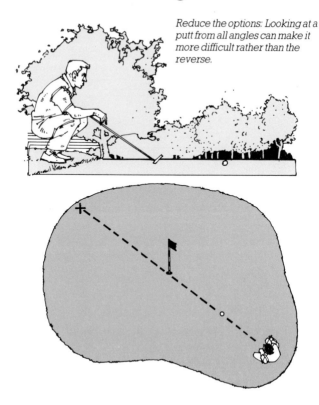

Reduce the options: Looking at a putt from all angles can make it more difficult rather than the reverse.

Diagnosis Many golfers line up a putt from behind the ball, from behind the hole and then from either side. Even the most advanced can sometimes fail to assimilate all this information to their advantage.

Treatment When Cathy Panton, daughter of the former World Senior Champion, John Panton, needed a 12-foot putt to finish second on her own in the 1988 St Moritz classic, she looked at the putt from behind and in front. When the lines she read conflicted, she remembered the words of her father: "Never look at a putt from more than the one angle because you can only get confused."

She opted for the first line she had seen and promptly made the 12-footer – a pressure putt if ever there was one – it was worth a little matter of $3,000.

Outlook Though you might feel the need to look at a long, 'cross-country' putt from a second angle, never feel tempted to do the same with a 4-footer. Nothing matters more with the short ones than that you should tackle them decisively.

HAZARDS

Guesswork from the rough

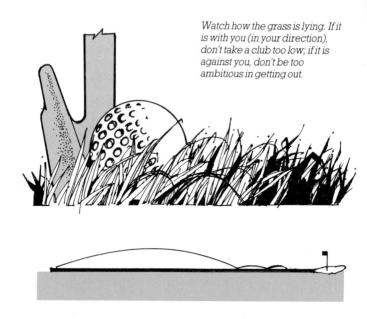

Watch how the grass is lying. If it is with you (in your direction), don't take a club too low; if it is against you, don't be too ambitious in getting out.

Diagnosis You have obviously never paused to consider such factors as the lie of the grass.

Treatment Your first concern, as Jack Nicklaus is apt to repeat, is to aim at playing your next shot from shorter grass. In other words, there is no point in being too ambitious.

If the grass is with you – lying in the direction of the green – you can afford to take a couple of clubs less than you would normally take for the distance.

Where you have the grass lying from left to right, you will need to aim a little left of target; on the same principle, when it is facing the other way you will need to aim a shade right. In other words, the ball will always tend to come out of the rough in the direction the grass lies.

Pro tip Seve Ballesteros, who plays trouble shots better than anyone, tries to take his club away slowly when he is in rough. That way he feels better placed to come up with the kind of aggressive follow-through needed to get his ball clear.

Imprisoned in rough

Thick rough can be a daunting sight. Practise swinging in the grass to build strength.

Diagnosis If you are a beginner, the sight of a ball nestling in long grass is ten times more daunting than it would appear to the player with trained hands and wrists.

Treatment The more balls you hit, the stronger you will get. To speed up the process, you could practise swinging an iron through long grass, trying all the time not to let your grip loosen. Don't be too ambitious.

Outlook When Marley Spearman, who won the British Women's Championship in 1961 and 1962, began in golf, she decided that she needed power in her arms similar to that in her legs (she had worked as a professional dancer). "As the hands are what link one to the club, it was obvious to me that they had to be strong."

To make up for the fact that she had "never lifted anything heavier than a teapot", Marley set about hitting a rolled-up carpet with an old club.

Sand storms

Diagnosis If, having taken the club back correctly, you fail to get out of a bunker at the first or second attempt, the chances are that you are doing one of the following:

a Lifting your head.

b Opening the face of your club to an extent where you are merely cutting right under the ball.

c Hitting the sand so far behind the ball as to have no impact on the ball itself.

Treatment Relaxation is one of the keys to successful bunker play. The sheer anxiety of whether or not the ball is flying clear causes heads to come up.

You must walk into a bunker with an assumption of success. Then, should you fail to get out at the first time of asking, you should leave the bunker before returning for a second attempt. Those few seconds will give you a little breathing space, time to gather your thoughts.

Outlook Pick up the rhythm of the professionals, by watching them live or on TV and, above all, never allow panic to set in.

Pro tip Nothing terrifies the beginner or the intermediate more than sand shots. But John Garner, probably the best teacher of golf in Britain, says that there is simply no reason to panic. He believes that even the hardest shot of them all, the plugged lie, can be played by the experts one handed, so what have you to worry about? Take an open stance, wriggle the feet for a firm base, aim at a spot an inch behind the ball and swing smoothly.

Stuck in a pot bunker

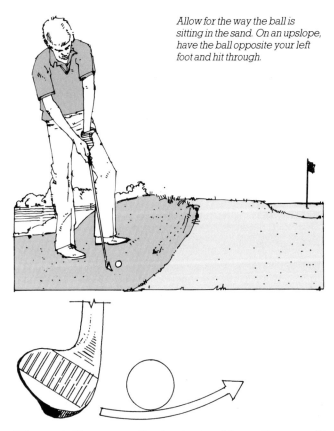

Allow for the way the ball is sitting in the sand. On an upslope, have the ball opposite your left foot and hit through.

Diagnosis You are not allowing for the different lies you will face in this type of trap: sidehill, uphill, downhill.

Treatment Remember that you must always swing with the slope. For example, when you are on an upslope, position the ball opposite or even just outside your left foot and hit up and through the ball. When you are on the downslope, you may hit down on the ball, never up.

Outlook Pot bunkers are usually found on a seaside course. However, even if you are not in the habit of playing on links, you are still going to get the occasional awkward lie in a conventional trap and it is as well to have the right antidote up your sleeve.

When you are in the back of a trap, there is no point in being over-ambitious. Laura Davies, in winning the 1987 U.S. Open, played one bunker shot – at Plainfield's short 12th hole – where she was content simply to hit from a bad lie at the back of a trap to an easier position at the front.

Too cleanly out of bunkers

Sand shuffle: Dig your feet into a
bunker to provide security and to
encourage the clubhead to take
its path through the sand.

Diagnosis You are probably not doing enough to achieve
the lower swing plane needed to take sand with the ball.
Apart from making a mental note as to how much of the sand
you will need to take behind the ball on any given shot, you
should look at your feet.

Treatment When you go into the trap, shuffle your feet into
the sand. This gives a sense of security and will automatically ensure a lower swing plane. This, of course, is applic-
able to those bunker shots where accuracy is all important.

When it comes to fairway bunker shots, such as the one
faced by Sandy Lyle at the final hole in the 1988 Masters at
Augusta, the last thing is to have the feet too deeply embedded in the sand. The reason is that you need to hit the
ball cleanly.

Outlook When playing away from home, make a point of
studying the texture of the sand. The last thing you would
want to say of any practice round is "I never went in a
bunker all day". Make a point of experimenting from both
fairway and greenside traps.

Lying among trees

In practice, acquire a range of shots by gripping down the shaft and keeping the hands in front.

Diagnosis You will always struggle until you have a handful of tried and tested escape shots at your disposal.

Treatment Take a few balls into the wooded area that troubles you most on your home course and experiment hitting over and under branches.

If you have no option but to hit low, grip your 2 or 3 iron well down the shaft and, positioning the ball towards your right foot, use a short swing and knock it out. By having the ball back in the stance, your hands will automatically be in front at the address – and that is where they must stay throughout the shot.

Should you need to shape the shot to the right, adopt an open stance (left foot a little back) and visualize the shot you want. By the same token, if your escape route asks for a right-to-left flight, stand a little shut.

Pro tip Seve Ballesteros's advice is that you should always look first for a high escape route. "Make sure," he warns, "that you choose a club with enough loft to get you back on the fairway."

Ball in bunker furrow

Go for a sharp pick-up and solid contact with the ball. Rake bunkers afterwards.

Diagnosis You need to be philosophical if you find yourself caught not just in a bunker but in a furrow or heel print. Getting out of such an indentation should not be too difficult, but it is a mistake to ask for too much.

Treatment Address the ball back in your stance, with the clubface a little closed and your hands ahead. Pick the club up abruptly and hit down hard behind the ball, without worrying too much about a follow-through. Little or no backswing will be imparted on this particular shot, so expect your ball to run a long way.

Outlook Make sure that you leave bunkers in good shape. It does not take long to educate an entire membership if a handful of people are prepared to set a good example by always raking.

Pro tip John Garner, former Ryder Cup player now devoted to teaching, was one of the finest short game exponents of his time. His advice for the most common of bad lies in a bunker, the plugged lie, is to take a normal stance with the ball in the middle of it, and then close the face of your sand wedge by at least 30 degrees. Pick the club up fairly abruptly on the backswing and chop down into the sand, never touching the ball.

Half in, half out

Play safe: If the ball is only just resting on sand, you cannot ground the club at the address. Err on the safe side if in doubt.

Diagnosis You need to decide what shot you are trying to play. If you are to play the stroke with any authority, you must treat it either as a bunker shot or as a fairway chip or pitch.

Treatment Where the terrain is unmistakably sandy, see the stroke as a bunker shot. Remember that, even if only a quarter of the ball is resting on sand, you are not allowed to touch the ground at the address. Indeed, whenever a bunker's border is ill-defined, you should err on the safe side and take pains not to ground your club.

Position your hands fractionally ahead of the ball and play your normal trap shot. However, since the usual tendency in this situation is to quit on the ball, think in terms of an easy swing with a full follow-through.

Outlook If you are aiming for a single-figure handicap you should make it a rule never to hit a ball without deciding precisely how you are going to play it and seeing the result you want in the mind's eye.

Lying in a ditch

*Keep still and rely on your hands
to play this, one of the most
difficult shots.*

Diagnosis You are attempting one of the hardest shots in golf and it may be better to pick out under penalty before you get yourself into worse trouble.

Treatment If you must play the shot – and we are assuming that the ball is in the ditch, that the ditch is a dry one and that you are having to stand on the bank – your only chance of success is to keep still and to rely on your hands to lead the clubhead to the ball.

The task will be made easier if there is room for you to stand in the ditch but, in this instance, you must ensure that you take a sufficiently lofted club to clear the bank.

Outlook If there is a network of ditches on your course and you are blessed with a real golfing eye, incorporate ditch work in your practice stints. This will familiarize you with the shot and enable you to spot at once the ball that can be extracted.

Lying in a divot

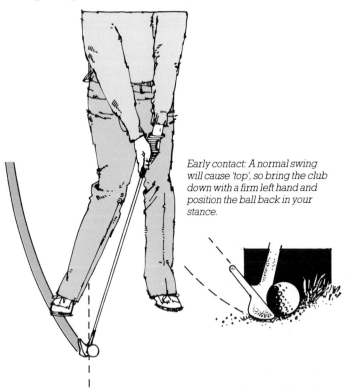

Early contact: A normal swing will cause 'top', so bring the club down with a firm left hand and position the ball back in your stance.

Diagnosis You have probably pampered yourself to the extent where nothing but the best lie is acceptable.

Treatment Your main thought, from a divot mark or bare ground, should be to make contact with the ball while the clubhead is still on the way down. Any attempt to sweep the ball up on the follow-through is likely to lead to your catching the ball on its head.

With a view to contacting the ball early, you should play it from a little further back in your stance. On the downswing, it will pay you to be conscious of a firm left hand and forearm.

Outlook You cannot afford to get too soft when playing winter rules. By always teeing up your ball on the fairway you will be unable to cope when, in competition, you have no option but to play the ball as it lies.

Parents will do their offspring's game more harm than good if they are forever suggesting that they should move a ball back on to the fairway or that they should select a flatter/better lie. Far better that young players should learn to improvise from the start.

Under water

Diagnosis You should not be contemplating hitting the ball from water if it is much more than an inch below the surface. If there is any doubt at all, you would do better to pick out under penalty.

Treatment If you are adamant about having a go, think twice before removing your shoes and socks and wading into the water. There have been countless stories of players treading on broken glass and cutting themselves in these circumstances.

Don't expect too much from your water shot. Water slows down the clubhead, so the best you can hope for is simply to get the ball back on to dry land.

Outlook If you are the type of golfer who cannot resist having a go, make a point of practising shots out of the edge of a water hazard. Get the feel of how the clubhead reacts in water: this is best experienced when you are experimenting rather than playing competitively.

Pro tip In Lee Trevino's experience, the best method is to hit 2 or 3 inches behind the ball: "That way, the force of the contact makes the ball jump up in the water. Your clubhead can catch it without having to cut so deeply".

Leafy lie

A bed of leaves may cause the ball to move at the address, which will cost a one-shot penalty. So keep the face open and don't risk grounding the club.

Diagnosis You have got to play the ball as it is and, since a bed of dried leaves can be a very springy base from which to play, you will need to be on the alert in case the ball moves as you address it. If this happens, you will incur a one-shot penalty.

Treatment Where you have an area of ground dotted with leaves and pine-needles, you can clean up around the ball if there is no danger of disturbing it. However, never feel tempted to ground your club at the address. For the short shot, have the ball forward in your feet and, with the club-face slightly open, explode from the leafy debris as you would from a bunker.

If you are looking for a longer shot, take one less club than you think you need in order to allow for the extra length which applies where you are unable to get a good grip of the clubface on the ball.

Outlook It is hard not to look up to see whether the shot has succeeded, but once that trick is mastered, this shot can be invaluable in 'rescuing' a score.

Hilly lies

Diagnosis Assuming that your course is not on the side of a hill, you should ask yourself if you are making full use of the flat land available.

Treatment Instead of going full throttle with your driver on a hole where, were you to hit the ball out of the middle, you would land on a downslope, take a 4 wood to ensure that you finish on flat land.

No less an authority than Jack Nicklaus has said that he would sooner be hitting a 5 iron from a flat lie than an 8 iron from one where he has a pronounced uphill or downhill lie.

On some courses, where money is short, you may often find yourself having to hit from a tee which is not entirely flat. If, after scouring the teeing area, you still cannot find a flat piece of land from which to tee off, bear in mind the difference a slope can make to the shape of your shot. If you are forced to stand with the ball above your feet, you will tend to draw the ball a fraction; where the ball is below your feet, expect a slight left-to-right flight.

Outlook A quick glance at the rules will show that you are not confined to teeing off on a line between the two markers. You can tee the ball up to two club lengths behind the markers, while you yourself can stand outside the markers provided that the ball is within the defined area.

WEATHER

Restricted by waterproofs

Diagnosis You may be happy enough in waterproof trousers but, like many other golfers, simply cannot get comfortable in the jacket.

Treatment Though long ago Abe Mitchell refused to be without a tight-fitting jacket on the grounds that his swing felt better under control, players of today have become accustomed to the freedom of playing in a sports shirt and sweater. If they want to feel comfortable playing in a water-proof jacket, they should practise in one.

Your best hope of finding an easy-to-wear top lies in selecting one which has elasticated cuffs and is of the pull-on variety rather than zip-up. Zips, in themselves, can be uncomfortably obtrusive, pouching out in all the wrong places.

Outlook If you cannot find anything suitable, buy the trousers and accept that you are going to get wet on top. Extra sweaters – two thin ones are always better than one thick one – will keep out all but the heaviest rain.

Sodden turf

Deal with sodden lies by picking the ball off cleanly; take one club more than you think you need.

Diagnosis You cannot have clean contact. Lee Trevino once likened hitting badly from soggy grass to playing out of mashed potatoes. The ball goes nowhere.

Treatment Trevino's recipe has always been to take a club more than he needs from drenched fairways. He chokes down on the shaft and swings a little more easily than he would normally. It is in choking down that he paves the way for hitting the ball cleanly instead of scooping it.

Putting on a wet green: the ball needs to be struck harder – not just to make the distance, but to hold its line.

Outlook Extra concentration, more than anything else, will help you keep your game together in adverse conditions. That apart, it is well worth being equipped with a towel, umbrella and an all-weather golf glove. Bear in mind that if you use ordinary golf gloves you could need as many as five or six on a really wet day. In such conditions, you may have to alter your pre-shot routine.

Pro Tip Greg Norman is in the habit of setting first one hand on the club and then the other. In the course of winning the 1986 Open, Norman had to adapt to putting both hands on the club almost at once, because his first hand was getting soaked before he added the second.

Struggling into head wind

To maintain length in wind, move the ball back in the stance and try a three-quarter swing to stay low.

Diagnosis Your mistake is becoming too rigid in the belief that this will help you in what you see as a battle against the elements.

Treatment Your normal swing can serve you perfectly well in a head wind – if you let it.

If you cannot afford to lose length at certain holes, position the ball a little further back in your stance in order to take the loft off your club at impact. Try for a three-quarter swing: if you make too free a swing and hit too hard, you could easily end up with exactly the kind of high shot you are trying to avoid.

Outlook Don't spend long hours on the practice ground in windy conditions as this could tear your swing from its habitual groove. However, it is worth experimenting on a calm day with the shot you would be looking for in a head wind.

Pro Tip Seve Ballesteros has the right attitude. He does not hang around waiting for the gusts to abate. Instead, he takes his usual practice swings and gets his shot away before the wind can affect stance and concentration. His only other concession is to grip the club a little more tightly than usual.

No control downwind

Full steam ahead: Take a lower club, hit a full shot and keep the turn full and free.

Diagnosis Playing downwind can often be more disconcerting than playing into wind.

Treatment Make the most of a downwind when you are on the tee by hitting a high ball. To do this, make a full turn and swing freely through the ball.

When it comes to playing your approach to the green, your instinct will tell you to hold back. However, you would do better to take a couple of clubs less than usual and hit a full shot. Your higher shot will have a more vertical descent and therefore a better chance of holding the green.

If the wind is slightly across, as well as down, you must resist the temptation to steer the ball in.

Outlook On the practice tee get into the habit of gauging the wind so that, for you, it is a 'one club' or 'two club' wind, and so on. If you hit a 6 iron, say, the distance you would normally hit a 4 iron, downwind, then it is a 'two club' wind. This helps enormously in judging distances.

Out in the cold

Keep the extremities warm, but don't be constricted. Wear plenty of layers.

Diagnosis Cold weather can be a problem throughout the year, especially if you play on a links or exposed hill course. This has been evident in recent Open Championships when television pictures have shown top professionals wrapped up and shivering in the cold.

Treatment As in wet weather it is important to keep warm without feeling constricted, so wear several layers of thin clothes rather than fewer thick ones. You must keep your extremities warm, especially your hands, feet and head. Try wearing ski gloves to keep your hands warm between shots and so retain feel. (Quality gloves can be expensive but the investment may be worthwhile.) Experiment with various textures of headgear to find the most comfortable for you. As with waterproofs, comfort is crucial to keep your swing and your spirits flowing.

Outlook Be prepared, like the boy scouts. Lee Trevino, after missing the halfway cut in the 1988 Open, said that Americans were not used to playing golf in poor conditions, and he joked that he had a limited wardrobe for bad weather. The lesson is to carry the necessary gloves, hats and extra sweaters in the bag at all times – even in summer.

MENTAL
APPROACH

MENTAL APPROACH
Inferiority complex

*Play the course; try to avoid your
playing partner. Acknowledge
his or her good shots, but don't go
overboard with praise.*

Diagnosis You are concentrating too much on your
opponent; not enough on playing the course.

Treatment While it is impossible not to be influenced by an
opponent's ball settling by the flag, don't let what he or she
is doing occupy your thoughts. Don't watch your opponent
hitting and, if he or she is exceptionally powerful, try to
avoid taking in the sound of the contact. Instead, you should
be warming to the prospect of being able to play your
second shot first.

Rather than watch, nervously, as an opponent tackles
putts, expect him to make them. That should stop you from
reacting badly at a time when you have your own putt to
ponder. Finally, acknowledge your opponent's good shots,
but don't go overboard in your admiration. By doing that you
will only give him confidence that you lack.

Outlook Remember, you only have to look as if you are
enjoying your golf to give an opponent the impression that
you can play.

No conviction

Imagine the best outcome for each shot and picture this in your mind.

Diagnosis You are probably approaching your shots with a picture of what you don't want to happen, rather than the reverse.

Treatment Try to see every shot in the mind's eye during your pre-shot routine. Picture the ball flying through the air and bouncing towards the hole. Similarly, when you are on the green, see your putt heading along the correct line and curling into the hole.

The reason for this is to give your mind and your body a well-defined task. Success never attends ill-defined objectives.

Outlook If you think about your ball ending up in sand or water, the error will be that much more likely to occur.

Too cautious

Go for it: The young Palmer and Nicklaus learned to give it a go. Control came later.

Diagnosis It is foolish to take too many risks; don't hit a difficult shot when there is an easier one you know how to play. However, you must remember that golf is essentially an attacking game. If you start holding back on your shots too much you will find yourself hitting the ball a glancing blow, which will cost you length and accuracy.

Treatment If you are a youngster starting out in the game, get into the habit of using your muscles and giving the ball a healthy whack. Jack Nicklaus and Arnold Palmer were always taught to hit the ball as hard as they could and neither regretted it, with Nicklaus insisting his sons did the same.

Outlook The chances are that you will not hit the ball as solidly or as accurately as you would like early on but, in time, harder hitting will pay off. You can always develop better control as you get older.

Pro tip Few people in golf have ever hit the ball as hard or as far as Jack Nicklaus. "The secret," he says, "is in not trying to hit it out of sight. When I want extra length I'll be sure not to hurry into the shot, not swing extra fast. I always make sure I complete the backswing."

Freezing over the ball

Freezing through tension may be cured by a pre-shot routine, but you can't hurry a cure.

Diagnosis This is a manifestation of tension.

Treatment Janet Collingham won the British Women's Championship of 1987 at Harlech at a time when she was freezing not just on her putts, but all her shots. There were times when she would look up as many as eight times before finally managing to take the club away. When it came to the 19th hole in her final, she took a full minute to pot the 9-inch putt she needed for the title.

Mrs Collingham did the right thing in not panicking. She knew all about her affliction, but refused to get it out of perspective, accepting that she would have to live with the gallery's disapproving whispers.

Pro tip Janet Collingham went for a chat with her professional, Brian Waites, when the match was over. He recommended a new pre-shot routine: last thing before taking the club away, Mrs Collingham was to exhale – in order to trigger the shot.

Irritated by hold-ups

Ignore your opponent's shots.
Remember he or she can draw
strength from your frayed nerves.
Waiting for others only adds to
your impatience, so find
something else to do. Aim to be
fresh when you tee up your shot.

Diagnosis You are too charged up for a game which is likely to take upwards of three hours.

Treatment You cannot afford to get irritated when the pace of a round is not going according to plan. Just as the kind of frayed nerves you get in a traffic jam are apt to cause accidents, so impatience on a golf course can play havoc with your score.

You will be most vulnerable when you find yourself having to wait for several players to tee off before you at a short hole. One thing you must never do in this situation is to watch their shots. Belle Robertson, former Curtis Cup player, once said that when she finds herself in this situation she will look at her feet, her golf bag, her watch – anything but the sight of other players' balls being thinned over the green or dispatched into sand. "I would want to be able to tee my ball up fresh," she explained.

Outlook Especially in match play, never let an opponent see that you are upset by such things. He or she will draw strength from your distress.

Blight of lost balls

It is safest to assume that you are the only person who cares where your ball finishes. So watch it.

Diagnosis You may be one of those golfers who assume that everyone else feels duty bound to keep an eye on your ball. Unless you are playing foursomes or fourball golf, it is safer to accept that you are the only person to whom the whereabouts of your ball really matters.

Treatment However hard you try to follow the line of your shot, you are still going to lose balls over the out-of-bounds fences, in gorse and in water. When it happens, and you have to make that long and often embarrassing walk back to play three off the tee, try to collect your thoughts.

If you are still seething, the chances are that you will merely duplicate the shot that has gone before. As Tommy Armour, 1931 U.S. Open Champion, once said, when you miss a shot don't think of what you did wrong. Approach the next shot thinking of what you must do right.

Outlook Parents can do their offspring a valuable service by not being too free with new golf balls. If new balls are too easily obtained, children will not bother to master the art of tracking them down in trees and rough.

Bad to worse

Forget the past: Learn to put a bad shot behind you, or your whole game will suffer.

Diagnosis You have probably made the age-old mistake of failing to put a bad shot behind you. By dwelling on that one mistake and wondering what on earth you have to do to repair the damage, you can find yourself in so acute a state of anxiety that one error turns into a string of disasters.

Treatment You must resist the temptation to put things right all at once. Bide your time until a realistic opportunity presents itself in which to pick up a birdie.

Outlook The often-repeated advice – play one shot at a time – is the best if you find it difficult to shrug off the effects of, say, a scuffed iron or a missed 3-footer.

Pro tip The words of Davis Love Jnr, who finished joint sixth with Jack Nicklaus in the British Open at Lytham in 1969, may be worth remembering: "Never look to follow a bad shot with a great shot. A good one will do just fine."

Rogue hole

Tackle a problem hole with a new plan. Go for the green with, say, three mid-irons instead of two woods.

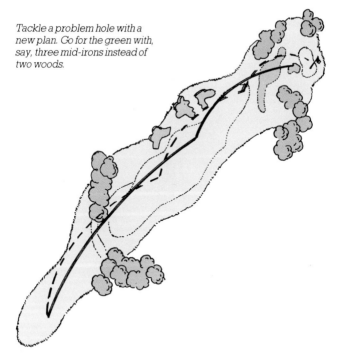

Diagnosis You have talked yourself into playing a particular hole badly, so that you approach it every time with negative thoughts.

Treatment If the hole has had you beaten for some weeks, the answer is to tackle it in an entirely different way.

It could be that you have been driving into the same fairway bunker every time. If this is so, leave your driver in the bag and opt instead for a 3 wood off the tee so that the bunker no longer comes into play.

At another hole where you have been hitting a drive and 9 iron, you would do better to settle temporarily for a 6 iron off the tee and a second 6 iron into the green. By doing that you will be asking entirely different questions of yourself, and your old problems will soon be forgotten. Only when you are back to playing the hole in par, or to your handicap, should you revert to your old clubbing sequence.

Where the rogue hole is a short one, stop aiming for the flag and choose a particular spot in the middle of the green.

Outlook Remember that a fresh approach can pay dividends when you get yourself into a rut. Don't give yourself the chance to get depressed or, alternatively, to take a perverse pleasure in a recurring golfing nightmare.

Conflicting thoughts

Swing free: Think of one key point during the swing. Too many will clog the mind.

Mind on fire: You may worry whether you are overswinging at the top...

...or simply that your swing is entirely in the wrong plane.

Diagnosis You may be trying to take in too much at once.

Treatment It is probably safer to have just one idea at a time. By concentrating on the one thing, your swing is that much more likely to keep its rhythm. It is easy to spot those who have too many technical thoughts: their swings give the impression of being divided into sections.

Joyce Wethered – who was rated by Bobby Jones, golf's best-ever amateur, as technically the best golfer, man or woman, he had seen – would thoroughly work out a technique on the practice ground, but deliberately cast aside all thoughts and theories before stepping on to the first tee. That way, she explained, she was free to concentrate on playing her match.

Pro tip Jack Nicklaus has said that he can cope with several swing thoughts at one time, but he believes the average golfer can only take on board a couple of key points.

Slow play

Think ahead: Work out the shot you intend to play as you walk up to your ball. Remember, too, to go to school on an opponent's putt.

Diagnosis If this is not an isolated complaint by someone who plays quickly, ask yourself if there is any truth in the suggestion.

Treatment Do you, for example, start thinking about each shot as you walk up to it, or do you only begin to apply yourself when you pull up alongside the ball? Do you stand idly by as your opponent putts, or do you spend that time working out your own line?

When you hit a bad shot, do you watch the flight of the ball? Do you watch your opponent's ball? Remember, it is much easier to follow it from the tee than to have to join in a search at the other end.

Remember to keep tabs on your own score and your opponent's so that you don't have to waste time going solemnly through each shot at the end of every hole.

Lack of impetus

Practice shots

Actual shot

Diagnosis You are thinking about your shots too long; or you are taking too many practice swings.

Treatment Where you have a long wait before play, don't pick up a club and begin your pre-shot routine before you must. However, you must be careful how you spend this spare time. You would, for instance, do better to check through your score card than chat to an opponent. That way you will hang on to your concentration.

It is easy to fall into the habit of taking too long over your shots. Former triple British women's champion Enid Wilson has often recommended, "Stand up and hit the thing". So take a couple of practice shots away from the ball; walk up to the shot from behind and hit it straight off.

Outlook Your shots will have more punch if impetus is not lost in the preliminaries. A feeling of excitement informs all the best hits.

Distractions

To keep your concentration intact before an important shot, you would do better to check your score card than to chatter.

Diagnosis It is very difficult to play and chatter at the same time. People will tell you that the likes of JoAnne Carner, who has won both the American women's amateur and Open championships, and indeed Lee Trevino, are happy to chat during a competitive round. But their conversations require little or no thought. They will say "Hello" and "Nice to see you" – but the chances are that they are probably not even registering to whom they are saying these things.

Treatment Don't get off on the wrong foot by chattering right up until your starting time. Take the opportunity of gathering your thoughts on the putting green.

On the course, you could follow the example of a number of professionals and confine your conversation largely to those first 50 yards as you walk off the tee. Your opponent or playing companion will soon get the message that you don't want to talk every inch of the way.

Outlook Make a point of confirming the state of the match, or your individual scores, at the end of every hole. Failure to do that can lead to unnecessary unpleasantness.

Standards slipping

New clubs for old: Modern weightings may help your quality of striking. As you get older, switch to lighter clubs, and don't expect to hit the ball as far as you did.

Diagnosis The time may have come to examine yourself and your golf. It could be that, at the age of 60, you are still intent on hitting everything as far as you did at 40.

Treatment Start taking a club more in order to dispense with the temptation to hit everything flat out. By doing this you can put the emphasis on accuracy.

Take a look, too, at your equipment. If you have been playing with the same clubs for ten to 15 years, the time may have arrived when you should switch to lighter clubs which will allow the clubhead to move faster through the ball with less effort.

Clubs of a more recent vintage could help with length and with quality of striking. For instance, the latest in heel-and-toe weighting will help a shot struck off-centre.

Outlook Unless you are especially attached to your old clubs, it is well worth trying a new set. They could give you a new lease of golfing life.

Frightened of water

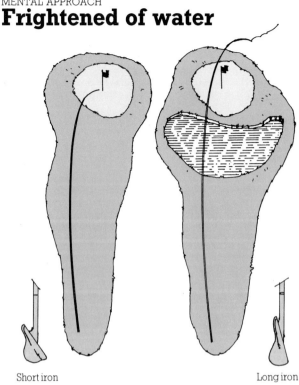

Short iron   Long iron

Diagnosis Your basic thinking is wrong. You forget that the 140-yard shot over water is precisely the same as the 140-yard shot over grass.

You are probably one of those who find an old ball every time you have to negotiate a particular water hazard. Again, you no doubt selected a club or two more than you needed to make certain of getting over the trouble.

Treatment All these precautions only leave your head awash with negative thoughts. By producing the old ball, you are saying to yourself that you are expecting the shot to disappear with a splash. Where your choice of club is concerned, if you hit it correctly you will go straight over the green; hold back on it and that is the best possible recipe for making a hash of the shot.

Take the right club for the yardage; see the shot for what it is.

Outlook A bit of mental toughness will stop you from getting such hazards totally out of proportion. If you have no option but to go over the water, put it to the back of your mind and focus instead on that part of the green where you will need to land if you are to get close to the hole.

Shy of trouble shots

Don't avoid tricky shots in practice. Working on them can build confidence.

Diagnosis You are not an experimenter.

Treatment Anyone should be able to develop a good enough repertoire of shots to be able to cope in most circumstances but, to be a real expert, you need to learn from the experience of Seve Ballesteros.

Seve, who started out in golf with an old and battered 3 iron, went on to play entire rounds from trees and rough, choosing all the wrong clubs and playing them from "the craziest places". The result was that he developed a proper understanding of trouble shots.

Outlook Don't avoid practising or hitting from trouble. For instance, when you are playing friendly golf, don't agree to play winter rules and tee your ball up everywhere.

Note for seniors The above advice is aimed at those setting out in golf, and although it is worth heeding, you have an excuse not to follow it to the letter. As Sir Henry Cotton, three times Open Champion, once said, senior citizens are entitled to make the game as much fun for themselves as possible. "Why not tee up in bunkers?" was one of the great man's cheerfully irreverent suggestions.

ADVANCED
PLAY

Difficulty achieving draw

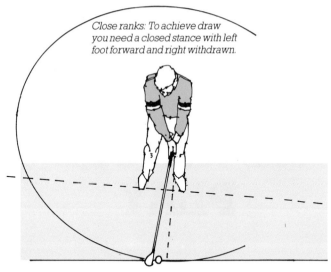

Close ranks: To achieve draw you need a closed stance with left foot forward and right withdrawn.

Diagnosis Though a natural golfer like Laura Davies, the 1987 U.S. Women's Open Champion, can produce a draw simply by seeing one in her mind's eye, you will need to make one or two technical adjustments to bring off this type of shot.

Treatment There are pros and cons in achieving a draw by altering the grip to show more knuckles on the left hand. It will work, but there are many – and they include Jack Nicklaus – who see it as too drastic an adjustment.

The best way to obtain a draw is by moving the ball a little further back and changing your stance. Start off by setting up to the ball as you would normally. Then move the right foot back a little off the target line, thereby giving yourself a closed set-up. If you were to draw a line between the right toe and the left, you would find yourself aiming right of target. All this will encourage the desired right-to-left spin on the ball.

Outlook The draw is not a shot you need to develop in your earliest golfing days. However, it adds length and is a useful shape of shot to have at your disposal on longer courses, especially into wind.

Pro tip Greg Norman, as befits the long-time number one golfer in the world, can play all the shots in the book and uses the drawn shot to emphasize his already enormous power and distance. He believes that the set-up is all important, and simply aims right, takes the club back on the inside and then makes sure that he comes back into the ball from the inside. "The more draw I want," he says, "the further right I aim. It's really very simple."

Difficulty achieving fade

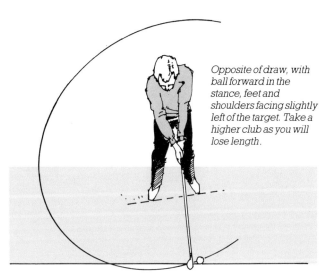

Opposite of draw, with ball forward in the stance, feet and shoulders facing slightly left of the target. Take a higher club as you will lose length.

Diagnosis Certain essentials are needed to produce the necessary out-to-in swing.

Treatment To fade the ball you will need to do precisely the opposite to what you would do for a draw (page 98). When you want to hit the ball from left to right, you should opt for an open stance. Feet and shoulders should be aligned to a point well left of target, thereby ensuring that the club will descend on the ball with the out-to-in swing.

The ball should be positioned slightly further forward in the stance than usual. It is worth experimenting with a more upright swing plane if you are having trouble in getting the right effect.

Though many golfers like to shape the ball from left to right, seeing it as a safe shot, it has to be remembered that the spin engendered will cost something in terms of distance. When so calling upon a deliberate fade, you will probably need an extra club.

Pro tip A controlled fade is what many of the best players aim for. Lee Trevino likes it because it lands softly, with less spin, than a hook. "You can talk to a fade," he says. He stands more open than is recommended, aims left and then, after taking the club back on the outside, drives through the ball with his left hand thrown at the target. With practice, that slice becomes a fade.

Shots too low

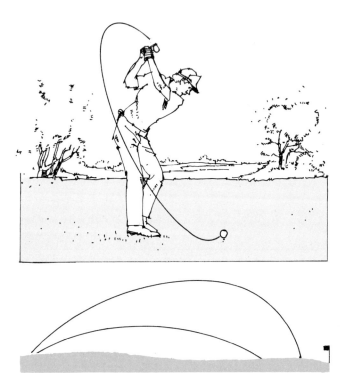

*Ensure that you are standing
close enough; and that your
hands can swing freely.*

Diagnosis This could be simply a question of getting ahead of the ball with your body. Alternatively, you could be standing too far from the ball and have developed too flat a swing in which hand action is stifled.

Treatment While a low trajectory could serve you well on a running, seaside course, you will find yourself in trouble when you get to lusher pastures. You will be effective into a wind with your lower flight, but you will never experience the thrill of cashing in on a following wind.

If you feel you are guilty of allowing your body to come through too soon, concentrate on making a better turn on the backswing and on hitting through with your hands.

If you sense that you are swinging flat, move closer to the ball and adopt a more upright swing plane. This will allow the hands to function more freely and pave the way for a higher flight.

Off turf or tee?

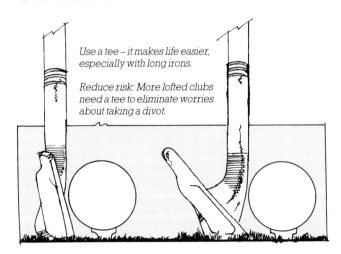

Use a tee – it makes life easier, especially with long irons.

Reduce risk: More lofted clubs need a tee to eliminate worries about taking a divot.

Diagnosis It is usually after watching the professionals that handicap golfers get it into their heads that hitting directly from turf is the thing to do at a short hole.

Many golfers are impressed by the casual brilliance with which some players – Laura Davies, Britain's best player, to name but one – drop the ball on the grass before hitting it to within a few feet of the flag.

Treatment The experts are agreed that you are losing a real advantage by failing to use a tee. Especially when you are wielding a low iron and looking for a powerful swing like the one you would use for your driver.

By teeing the ball, even if it is only just above the turf, you will get cleaner club-ball contact. There is less chance of catching an uneven spot on the turf or worrying about taking a divot.

Outlook Always make the game as simple as possible for yourself. In addition to using a tee-peg, make sure you tee your ball on that side of the tee which opens up the fairway.

Pro tip Tommy Armour, 1931 U.S. Open Champion, once warned: "Tee up your ball thoughtlessly on all or most of the 18 holes, and you are liable to produce a horrifying addition to your score."

Swaying into trouble

Motion creates commotion: A sway of more than a few inches will disturb both balance and swing. Keep in check.

Diagnosis You may have wrongly assumed that extra movement of your body will give you more length.

In moving away from the ball – anything more than a 6-inch lateral movement comes into the sway category – you will have trouble in getting your weight back into the shot.

Treatment While many professionals now stress that the head does not have to be kept statue still, you should not put too liberal an interpretation on this instruction. Curtis Strange, the 1988 U.S. Open Champion, has a slight sway, while Japan's Chako Higuchi succeeded in becoming one of the world's top women professionals with a hugely swaying swing. However, in order to keep that action intact, she had to practise for long hours every day.

The victim of a destructive sway should try hitting shots on the practice ground with the feet close together.

Once back on the course, the golfer should return to his or her normal stance but resist the temptation to hit the ball too hard. In other words, play well within your limits until the sway is safely out of your system.

Pro tip Gary Player has always recommended that the chronic swayer should hit a bucket of practice balls with his right foot turned in – a manoeuvre which should promote the feeling of being locked into a set position.

Overswinging

Avoid turning too far. Sam Snead advised playing barefoot as a natural antidote to an unwieldy action.

Diagnosis Though the studs in your shoes are there primarily to stop you from slipping as you make your swing, you are using them – perhaps unwittingly – to help you make an exaggerated turn. Without studs, you would probably be falling over.

Treatment By way of an experiment, try playing in a pair of tennis shoes. Legendary American professional Mickey Wright won several of her 82 titles on the Ladies Professional Golf Association tour in this type of footwear.

Alternatively, you could emulate Sam Snead, winner of seven major championships, and hit some shots barefoot. Snead played much of his early golf in bare feet and, in answer to a bet, once went barefoot at Augusta and got round in 68.

That he had drawn attention to himself in such a way made him less than popular. However, the fact that he had scored as he did had him analysing the advantages of playing without shoes.

Pro tip Sam Snead said that in studded shoes he had been swinging too hard and fast. His barefoot action was one which automatically made him play well within his limits – "at 75 per cent, I should say, of my full power."

Worried by caddie

Make sure that a caddie will look after you quickly, quietly and efficiently.

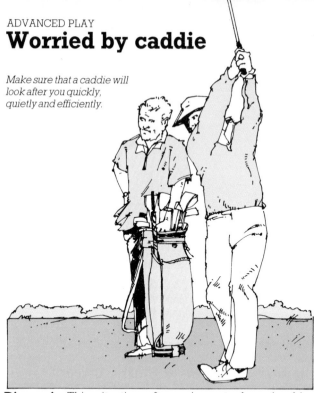

Diagnosis This situation often arises at championships where club members and other locals, often with the best of intentions, offer to act as caddies for the contestants. Sometimes it works well, but there are occasions when it can be disastrous for a competitor's concentration.

Treatment If you do accept the offer of help, it is only fair at the outset that you make clear the conditions under which you prefer to play. A quick explanation as to how you prefer to walk, and whether or not you like to chatter, will save untold embarrassment.

There was a typical caddie-player conflict during the 1988 St Moritz Classic. At about the third hole in her second round, the eventual winner, Janice Arnold, of New Zealand, was confronted by a man from the crowd who insisted on pulling her trolley. She accepted and, only minutes later, was regretting that decision because he was lagging 50 yards behind.

The more she asked him to hurry the more, it seemed, he dropped behind. A decision had to be taken and, on the eleventh tee, she bravely snatched her clubs and made off without him. He got the message – and she went on to recover her concentration and win.

Outlook A golden rule for anyone carrying another's bag is never to offer advice unless it is specifically requested.

Strained wrists and arms

Practice is important, but it can also lead to strains. Watch for the first sign of trouble and be prepared to take a rest.

Diagnosis You have been putting in too much practice off hard ground. Persistent jarring causes a form of tennis elbow.

Treatment The time to stop practising is when you feel the first twinge of discomfort. If you persist, you could end up out of the game for some months. Golfers' tennis elbow has claimed many victims among golfers in recent years. A splint is available which can prevent the condition from becoming worse but, in addition to wearing this support, you should start hitting all your practice shots from a tee-peg.

Back and wrist injuries were seldom a factor when professionals played only a handful of tournaments over the season. Now men and women professionals alike are playing week-in, week-out and, as a result, there is much more strain on their bodies.

Outlook Quality rather than quantity should be emphasized in youngsters' practice sessions. They should have it dinned into them that slogging away on the practice ground is not the only road to improvement. Time should be devoted to course management.

Confused on 'gimme'

Diagnosis A 'gimme' is a putt close enough to give; but it is difficult to define. The best explanation of how to decide when and when not to give a putt came from Susan Shapcott, an 18-year-old member of the Great Britain and Ireland team which won the 1988 Curtis Cup match against the Americans at Royal St George's.

Asked why she so often asked the Americans to hole short putts, Shapcott replied: "I never give putts I don't fancy myself."

Treatment Before any match play fixture, make a point of holing out all the little putts that your golfing friends would put in the 'gimme' category. In the match itself, expect to be asked to hole the shorter putts. If you spend time wondering whether or not such and such a 2½-footer is going to be given, you are merely creating the kind of atmosphere in which you might miss.

If you do miss, don't get obviously annoyed. You will give your opponent still more of a boost.

Outlook You will meet, in the course of time, players who will give 2-foot putts at the start of a round, but then, as the match gets tight, suddenly refuse them, hoping that your lack of recent practice, plus the pressure, will make you miss. Being prepared for this will help to hole them.

PRACTICE

Unsatisfactory session

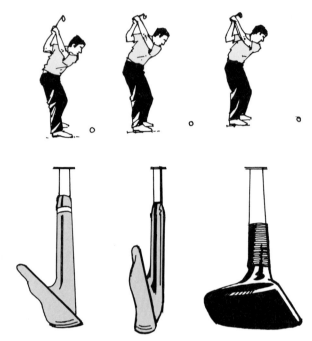

Plan of action: Warm up gradually before finding rhythm with more lofted clubs (left). Think it through: Tackle long irons and woods when warm, and always finish sessions with straightforward shots.

Diagnosis Your practice probably lacks organization.

Treatment Even if you were striking your 4 iron badly on the previous day, there is no case for going out and hitting an isolated cluster of 4 irons by way of preparation for your next round.

You should have a set plan for your session; one which allows you to warm up gradually. Start off with a few bends and stretches and from there proceed to a few half wedges or 9 irons. Once you have found your rhythm with these clubs, you can then move on to the longer irons and woods.

Towards the end of a session try a few of the specialist shots you might need. Always try to finish up with some straightforward shots so you head for the first tee with your swing in a groove.

Outlook You should always practise concentration as well as ball hitting. Don't ever make the mistake of going to the practice ground either with a portable radio, or, worse, headphones.

Practice makes imperfect

Putting plan: Bring method to your practice in ever-increasing circles. Put 2- to 6-footers first.

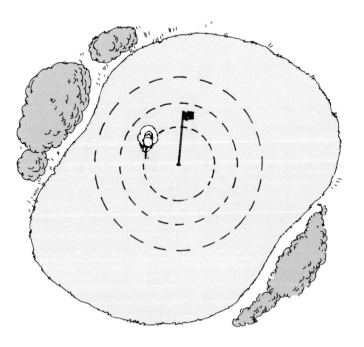

Diagnosis You are practising without a plan. Too many golfers go round and round the practice putting green but fail to achieve anything in terms of schooling themselves.

Treatment Walter Travis, the man who introduced the centre-shafted putter to Europe, was one of the first professionals to bring method into his putting practice. Though he would spend plenty of time practising the 25- to 30-footers, trying to hit them within 3 feet of the hole, he concentrated more on the 2- to 6-footers.

He would begin with the 2-footers, placing each of his four balls north, east, south and west of the hole. Then, having knocked in those four, he would move on to the 3-footers, the 4-footers and so on. However, if any one of the putts missed, he would happily start the whole procedure all over again.

Outlook Though the type of putting practice outlined above is demanding, it obviously pays to develop a set syllabus. That way you will get a clearer idea of whether you are making progress.

Practice swing better than play

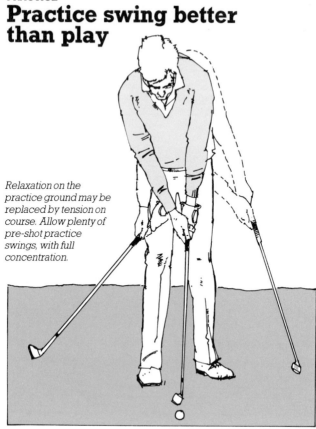

Relaxation on the practice ground may be replaced by tension on course. Allow plenty of pre-shot practice swings, with full concentration.

Diagnosis The reason swings tend to look better without the ball than with is that the golfer in question is relatively relaxed. When it comes to hitting the ball, the less confident competitor automatically shows signs of tension.

Treatment This is not to say that the golfer would do better to dispense with a practice swing. One practice swing is enough when you are playing a tee shot or any shot where you are hitting the ball the full distance. However, when it gets down to the half or three-quarter shot, you will need two or even three practice swings, the reason being that you have got to marry the right length of swing to the distance. It is almost as important to have your concentration at full stretch for the practice swings as it is for the shot itself. Without proper rehearsal, you cannot hope for concise and confident contact.

Outlook Don't overdo pre-shot routines. If you have too many practice swings and preliminaries, you will be in danger, when it comes to competition golf, of being warned for slow play.

Driving ranges

It may be difficult to find a club to join in your area. Waiting lists are often long and, if this is so, you can get a head start by making frequent visits to a local driving range.

Quality rather than quantity should be your guiding principle on the range. If you get stuck into a bucket of balls and hit them straight off, the chances are that you will be hitting the ball rather worse at the finish than you were at the start. You are asking too much of your hands and arms.

Hit a few shots at a stretch. And, every time you take a break, check that your alignment is correct. To do this, lay a club across your toes and then check from behind that it is facing in precisely the intended direction.

Far too many golfers at driving ranges make the mistake of hitting balls into the field without taking aim on a specific target. This encourages sloppy play and renders the session pointless.

Many driving ranges have par-three courses or pitch and putt areas attached. Don't scoff at these miniature versions of the real thing. The deeper you get into the game of golf, the more you will appreciate the importance of little pitches and putts.

It is on small courses such as these that you will see

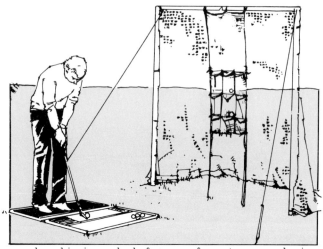

people achieving a deal of success from stances and grips that look horribly contorted. Such methods may serve people well enough at this level but, if you want to progress, you would do better to take pains to get yourself technically correct from the start.

In some cases, if you have fooled around at the game for some time, you may need to get worse before you get better. It is worth it. If you know yourself to be a bad stylist, don't succumb to the temptation to take your offspring up to the driving range with you. They will probably imitate the way you play.

It would be better if you could first pay for them to have a couple of lessons with a professional. He can give them the correct picture of how they should be swinging the club.

Going to a driving range will not have miraculous results. A Scottish housewife, one cold winter, went twice a week to golf evening classes at a local school where there were facilities in the gym for hitting from mats into nets.

The young professional taking the classes insisted she was coming along well – so much so that, when the classes ended and a friend offered to take her up to the golf club for a first time, she was bursting with excitement and confidence. However, she found the golf course game altogether different.

In the first place, the ball was not being teed up as had been the case at the evening classes and she was no longer hitting off uniformly flat ground.

Her golf that day was a complete let-down. She handed back her borrowed clubs and never played again. The point of this story is to illustrate how important it is that you should not get *too* used to hitting in driving range conditions. There must be some place where you can get the taste of the real game and practise hitting from the turf.

RULES
&
GLOSSARY

Rules

All too many golfers cannot be bothered to study the rules until they have been involved in an incident. This may be resolved easily enough, but then the golfer often returns to a blissful state of ignorance. This can lead to an uneasy atmosphere between players.

It is essential that all golfers obtain a copy of *The New Rules of Golf* from their professional before taking part in a competitive round. The rules are basically common sense and it is not necessary to know them by heart. But it is important that players are sufficiently familiar with the contents to know where to find a relevant piece of information.

The rules were revised in 1984, when they were slightly reduced in number (from 41 to 34). The opening section is perhaps the most crucial, because it deals with etiquette. Golf's long-established association with common courtesy has helped to protect it from the outbursts of ill-temper and general abuse which afflict other sports.

The early section of the rules on etiquette makes it clear that golfers should play without delay, but not when the players in front are in range; and without talking, moving or standing too close to someone taking a shot.

Another clear directive in the section on etiquette is often abused by club golfers: that players searching for a lost ball should not let the statutory five minutes pass before allowing the group playing behind to go through. A group which is lagging behind must also give way to the players following.

Above all, the rules are designed to make golf a game which moves reasonably rapidly. All golfers, whether they play off scratch or are novices, should mind their manners and prevent a whole course of people from being trapped in a five-hour traffic jam.

They should also note the sections on replacing divots, raking bunkers, and mending tees and greens which they have damaged. In short, don't be selfish.

Basic rules

Rule 1 makes it all seem so simple: *The Game of Golf consists in playing a ball from the teeing ground into the hole by successive strokes in accordance with the Rules.*

People who break a rule are usually penalized by losing two shots in stroke play or a hole in match play. Before you set off, there are regulations about the ball, the club and the grip.

Of course, you are not allowed more than 14 clubs in your bag. The penalty for breaking this rule is disqualification. So count your clubs before teeing off.

Make sure that you take your tee shot from the right place: between, not in front of, the markers provided. In match play, a player breaking this rule may be asked to take the shot again.

The ball must generally be played where it lies. The exceptions are if it is stuck in its own pitchmark; it may also be replaced if it is lying in casual water, on marked ground under repair, or in a hole or scrape made by a burrowing animal. In such cases, the ball is dropped within two club lengths of where it lies; these days from an outstretched hand held at shoulder height.

There must be another drop if the ball finishes nearer the hole than it originally lay, or hits the player's bag. If it rolls into a hazard, that is tough luck.

If, for any other reasons than those specified above, a ball is deemed unplayable, you can try to get relief by dropping, but that costs a stroke.

You are not allowed to improve the area round the lie of the ball. Trees and bushes can only be broken or bent in taking up a natural stance and playing the shot, although you are allowed to remove loose impediments, such as stones or twigs. This does not apply in a hazard, where the club may not be grounded at the address.

This rule about playing the ball where it lies led to a notorious incident in the 1983 World Match Play Championship at Wentworth. Britain's Nick Faldo had a wayward ball thrown back on to the 16th green by a spectator. Despite protests, Faldo was allowed to play the ball where it lay on the green, because the referee could not say that it had come to rest before being unfairly returned. Usually, the help given to tournament players by spectators accidentally getting in the way is not so blatantly unfair.

On the green, there are some variations because you are allowed to repair pitchmarks (but not the holes made by spikes). You cannot touch the line of your putt. If your ball is in the way of an opponent, it must be marked according to a set procedure. If you leave your ball above ground on the lip of the hole, you cannot wait *more than a few seconds* to see if it will drop.

In competition, take special care about start times and signing your card. Lateness or mistakes can lead to disqualification. If you sign for more strokes than you have taken, that total has to stand.

The rules are ultimately enforced by the Royal and Ancient or their appointee (either a referee or the local committee). Some odd rulings have been recorded.

In the late 1970s, for example, a letter arrived at the Ladies Golf Union (L.G.U.) from a women's committee. It told of a member who, after nine holes, had 'entered the clubhouse, bought a drink at the bar, consumed same, and then returned to the tenth tee and completed her round'.

The L.G.U. seemed less interested in the fact that the woman in question had been drinking than whether she had caused a hold-up. They ruled: 'Since you make no reference to any delay, it was quite in order for the member to enter the clubhouse'.

In another case, one club member was dominating local competitions to such an extent that the local committee asked the authorities if they could limit one competitor to one prize each year. The reply was that a committee could make their own rules about prizes awarded.

The rules can sometimes be open to individual interpretation, and the Royal and Ancient are the final arbiters. But ignorance is never an excuse for an offender.

Mr X v Mr Y: a short case history

To give some idea of the pitfalls in the rules out on the course, let us follow a couple of golfers, Mr X and Mr Y, for three holes of match play.

At the first hole, the two men hit their balls side by side in an area of light rough. After X has hit his second, Y announces that he must have hit the wrong ball. The ruling is to be found under Rule 15-2:

If a player plays a stroke with a wrong ball except in a hazard he shall lose the hole.

In other words, X goes one down immediately. Had this been stroke play, incidentally, X would have incurred a penalty of two strokes unless the only stroke or strokes played with the ball were played when it was lying in a hazard.

At the second hole, Y discovers that his drive has rolled into a cavity among tree roots and decides that his wrists will be at risk if he attempts to hack it out. In this instance, Rule 28 comes into play:

At any place on the course except in a water hazard, a

player may declare his ball unplayable. The player is the sole judge as to whether his ball is unplayable. If the player deems his ball to be unplayable, he shall, under penalty of one stroke:

a *Play his next stroke as nearly as possible at the spot from which the original ball was last played or moved by him (see Rule 20-5);*
  or
b *Drop a ball within two club lengths of the spot where the ball lay, but not nearer the hole;*
  or
c *Drop a ball behind the spot where the ball lay, keeping that spot directly between himself and the hole, with no limit to how far behind that spot the ball may be dropped.*

Y chooses option **b** and hits his third shot into a greenside bunker. X, who is waiting a little impatiently beside the green, sees that his opponent's ball has come to rest against a stray branch that has probably been dragged into the trap by children.

In a move to speed things up, he goes into the bunker and moves the branch, thereby improving the lie of the ball. By so doing, he has helped Y rather more than he believed to be the case for, under Rule 1-2:

No player or caddie shall take any action to influence the position or the movement of a ball except in accordance with the Rules.

The penalty in match play is, as usual, loss of hole; in stroke play, two strokes.

The golfers are now all square and, in order to establish a winner in this somewhat ill-fated contest, we will call the next hole the decider. In a trouble-free interlude, the players arrive on the green in three shots apiece.

At this point, Y notices that his ball is no longer round. He has watched a good deal of golf on television and has several times seen top professionals changing their golf balls when they get on to the putting surface.

He takes it upon himself to do that, but he has not referred to Rule 5-3:

If the player lifts the ball without announcing his intention in advance or giving his opponent, marker or fellow-competitor an opportunity to examine the ball, he shall incur a penalty of one stroke.

That little slip costs him the hole and the match. Where the reader is concerned, the hope is that this tale will make him realize that to be equipped with common sense is not quite enough.

There is no more essential piece of equipment than the book of rules.

Glossary

Address   The stance from which a player hits the ball. In terms of *The New Rules of Golf*, a player is said to have addressed the ball once he or she has adopted the stance and grounded the club behind the ball. If the player is in a **hazard** he or she is not permitted to ground the club.

Albatross   A score at an individual hole which is three shots below the **par** – i.e. a two at a par five.

Alignment   The player's set-up in relation to where he is aiming.

All Square   A level match.

Amateur   A golfer who plays for fun rather than money. Vouchers can be played for in the amateur game, but there is a ceiling on their value which is adjusted from time to time by the Royal and Ancient, the body in charge of the amateur game.

Baffy   The name once given to the equivalent of today's 3 or 4 wood.

Birdie   A score at an individual hole which is one below **par** – i.e. a two at a par three.

Blind hole   A hole where the golfer cannot see his or her target.

Bogey   Once the term applied to a **par** but today used to describe a score that is one over the par of the hole.

Borrow   To allow for the natural roll on the putting green. The amount of borrow depends to no small extent on the speed of the putt.

Bunker   Holes in the ground filled with sand and placed on points of the course where they will catch stray shots. Bunkers will vary in depth; some will demand that the player opens the face of the sand wedge in order to get the necessary height to escape, while there are others from which the ball can be putted clear. It is up to the golfer who goes into a bunker to tidy up with the rake provided.

Caddie The man or woman who carries the player's clubs. Under *The New Rules of Golf*, the caddie is permitted to advise the player, he or she is seen as part 'of the side'.

Carry That area of water, heather or **rough** which must be carried before the player reaches the **fairway.**

Casual water Water appearing on the **fairway** after a downpour would come under the rules' definition of casual water. See *The New Rules of Golf*, Rule 32.

Chip A little shot hit with a short swing, usually on to the green. The player would also chip clear of trouble – i.e. from trees back on to the **fairway.**

Concede Giving a hole to the opposition when all hope of a win or **half** has disappeared. On the putting green a simple putt would be conceded.

Divot The wad of turf which comes up with an iron shot where the player has hit down on the ball. Divots will be taken unintentionally by beginners unable to judge that point at which they should be making contact with the ball.

Dogleg Holes where there is a change in direction. The good player will often be faced with a decision as to whether or not he or she should play over trees in order to make the hole shorter.

Dormie Used in match play to describe a situation where, if the match is only over 18 holes, a player cannot be beaten. If, for example, he is three up with three to play, he is dormie three.

Drive The first **stroke** at a hole. The drive from the first **tee** is the shot which Jack Nicklaus insists matters more than any other in that it can often dictate how a golfer is going to play for the rest of his round.

Drop Under *The New Rules of Golf*, players are

commonly forced to drop a ball. The drop can be introduced when a ball is lost or knocked into a water **hazard.**

Duck hook A shot bearing a more than usually pronounced **hook.**

Duff A mis-cued shot.

Eagle The term apparently came into use in 1922 to describe a score two shots under the **par** for the hole – for example, a three at a par five.

Eclectic competition A competition in which two or more rounds of **stroke** play are held, with the golfer having to count only his best score from each hole. Eclectic competitions are often run over winter stretches because, with the odd bad hole not mattering too much, players can get more enjoyment in difficult conditions than they might from straight forward **medal** events.

Fade A shot which fades away to the right, otherwise known as a **slice.**

Fairway That area of mown grass between **tee** and green.

Fat When the player makes contact with ground too far before the ball.

Fore The golfer's cry when he or she has hit a ball which is in danger of hitting other people on the course.

Fourball A match involving four players, each one of whom will hit his or her own ball.

Foursome A match involving four people in which two play together and hit alternate shots. This is one of the oldest forms of golf and is played seldom outside Great Britain.

Freeze A state of nerves: the player is unable, say, to take the putter away. He or she will be said to be freezing over the ball.

Gimme A shortening of 'Give me', applied to putts

too short to be missed.

Grip   The position of the hands on the club; the position of the hands on the bound area at the top of the shaft of a club.

Groove   A swing in the groove is one which has the virtue of repeating.

Ground under repair   Typically, an area where new grass seed has been sown, from which a player may **drop** his or her ball without penalty.

Half   A hole where opponents make the same score.

Half shot   Where the player does not employ a full swing. The golfer may, for example, prefer to hit a half 6 iron instead of a full 8 iron in order to keep the ball down under the wind.

Hazard   *The New Rules of Golf* describes a hazard as any bunker or water hazard.

Homeward half   The back nine.

Honour   The player who hits first from the **tee** has the honour. After the first hole, where the player at the top of a draw sheet would tee off first, the honour will go to the player who won the previous hole. Where a hole is halved, the honour will remain with the person who last won a hole.

Hook   A shot which starts straight, but turns left in mid-flight.

Impact   The moment at which club strikes ball.

In play   A ball is said to be in play from the moment the player tees off until the moment it is in the hole; unless it is lost, lifted, ruled **out of bounds** or substituted under *The New Rules of Golf*.

Lie   How the ball comes to rest. For example, a ball which finishes in a footprint in sand will be termed a bad lie.

Line The intended route of a shot.

Links Seaside courses with natural seaside features such as sand-dunes.

Lip Edge of hole. The player will talk about the ball having come to rest on the lip of the hole.

Medal play A competition in which all **strokes** are counted. Unlike in match play, no putts can be **conceded.**

Nap The grain of the grass on the green. It can affect the roll of the ball, the putt *with* the nap travelling further than the putt *against* the nap.

Net score The score after a player's handicap has been deducted.

Nineteenth The first extra hole where a match is still undecided after 18 holes. The '19th hole' is a term also used to describe the club bar.

Out of bounds A shot hit into an out-of-bounds area as defined on the card of the course.

Outside agency Any person on the course who is not actually playing. The term can also apply to, say, a piece of machinery or an animal. Whenever an outside agency moves a ball, the ball can be replaced without penalty. If the outside agency is seen to make off with the ball, another can be substituted.

Pacing 'Pacing the course' or 'taking yardages' are phrases applied to players planning their way around a course.

Par The par of a hole represents the score a first-class golfer could be expected to make under normal weather conditions.

Pin high A shot which has stopped neither short nor past the pin, but level with the hole.

Placing Improving the **lie** of the ball in winter conditions in accordance with local rules. Players who agree among themselves to place the ball in their friendly games can often find it difficult to return to playing the ball as it lies.

Play through   To overtake players in front who may, perhaps because of a lost ball, have lost ground.

Plugged ball   A ball which is embedded either in wet ground or in a bunker. Unless a local rule applies, the ball must be played as it **lies.**

Plus   A player with a handicap better than **scratch** is said to have a plus handicap.

Practice swing   A rehearsal swing which will give the player the feel of what he is trying to do. There is no restriction on the number of practice swings a player may take, but there is a penalty for undue delay of two **strokes.**

Push   A shot that is hit right of target.

Quitting   Easing up on a shot, a failure to hit firmly through the ball.

Rabbit   A poor player; beginner.

Rap   A firm, concise means of hitting a putt.

Rough   Unmown grass flanking **fairway,** indeed all around the fairways, **tees** or greens.

Rub of the green   Anything that happens to the ball accidentally while it is **in play** – for example, the ball bouncing off an on-course tractor on to the green.

Run-up   Term used to describe a little running shot hit to the green with a less than normally lofted club.

Scratch golfer   A player who has a handicap of nought.

Semi-rough   Area of half-cut grass between **rough** and **fairway.**

Set   A full set of clubs, 14 being the maximum number permitted.

Shank A shot which comes off that area on the club where shaft joins blade. The ball shoots off to the right.

Slice The carving of a ball out to the right. Instead of hitting the ball squarely, the clubhead will have come across the ball from right to left.

Smother The ball is hit into the ground as opposed to up in the air.

Socket Another term for a **shank**.

Stableford A system of scoring where the player gets one point for a **bogey**, two for a **par,** three for an **eagle** and so on. A popular form of golf at club level in that the player will not be destroyed by the odd bad hole.

Stroke A term used instead of shot. It is also applied in the handicapping system when the better player, the one with the lower handicap, gives a shot or shots to his higher handicap opponent.

Sway Used to describe a swing wherein the golfer sways away from the ball on the backswing, failing to keep his or her head steady over the ball.

Take-away The first movement of club away from ball on the backswing. A jerky take-away will affect the rhythm of the swing as a whole.

Tee The peg on which the ball is placed for a drive. It can be of wood or plastic. Also, the area from which the teed ball is driven.

Tempo Rhythm, timing.

Thin A ball hit from the bottom of the club. The shot will sound wrong and the ball will fly low.

Top To hit the ball above centre, the result being that it jumps along the ground.

Topspin A ball hit with topspin revolves in a

downward direction while in flight. It rolls on landing. Topspin is imparted automatically with the flatter-faced woods.

Twitch

A term to describe the convulsive jerk made at a short putt by the player who has lost confidence.

Underspin

Underspin is applied to the ball by hitting it below the centre.

Upright swing

One in which the player takes the club away steeply as opposed to swinging away on a flat plane.

Waggle

Lifting the club up and down prior to the **take-away,** the idea being to impart life to the start of the swing. Where there are no preliminaries, the player is often apt to jerk the club back at the start of his or her swing.

Index

Acknowledgements

The assistance of Nicholas Keith in creating *Golf Clinic* is acknowledged with gratitude.

Illustrations	**Michael McGuinness**
Art director	**Mel Petersen**
Design assistance	**Chris Foley and Beverley Stewart**
Editorial director	**Andrew Duncan**
Proofreading	**Laura Harper**
Index/editorial assistance	**Rosemary Dawe**